The Philosopher's Stone presents text and analysis of three major alchemical works, approached symbolically, using the symbol systems and viewpoints of magic and psychology. The objective of alchemical study has been described poignantly by the author:

> *Like modern psychological methods the alchemical formulae have as their goal the creation of a whole man, of integrity.... Not only does Alchemy envisage an individual whose several constituents of consciousness are united, but with the characteristic thoroughness of all occult or magical methods it proceeds a stage further. It aspires towards the development of an integrated and free man who is illumined. It is here that Alchemy parts company with orthodox Psychology.*

The clarity and elegance of the author's style and the precision and depth of his thought make *The Philosopher's Stone* an important and meaningful experience for every person who aspires to personal development and wholeness.

THE PHILOSOPHER'S STONE

A modern Comparative Approach to Alchemy from the Psychological and Magical Points of View

ISRAEL REGARDIE

Second Edition
Revised and Enlarged

Alchemy *is* philosophy; it is *the* philosophy, the seeking out of the *Sophia* in the mind.

1970
LLEWELLYN PUBLICATIONS
Saint Paul, Minnesota 55165, U.S.A.

Copyright © 1970 by Llewellyn Publications

First Edition 1938
Second Edition Revised 1970
Second Printing 1974

Llewellyn Publications
Post Office Box 3383
Saint Paul, Minnesota 55165

International Standard Book Number: 0-87542-691-3 (paper)

Printed in the United States of America

DEDICATION

It gives me enormous satisfaction to dedicate this new
edition to
                    Frater Albertus Spagyricus
who, benevolently and sagaciously, has opened my eyes to
the further meanings of Alchemy.

INTRODUCTION TO SECOND EDITION

During the winter of 1936-37, while living in London, I came down with a severe cold which proved intractable to treatment. My respiratory tract had become sensitized in early childhood by a bout of bilateral bronchial pneumonia. The result was that I was confined to bed for two weeks.

Instead of the usual mystery and detective stories recommended for such situations, my reading companion was Mrs. Atwood's *Suggestive Inquiry into the Hermetic Mystery.* For years I had struggled vainly with this large tome, annoyed continually by its obscurantism and pompous literary style that was almost as bad as A. E. Waite's, but I had never really managed to comprehend her presentation of Alchemy. Now, bedridden, I was determined to give her book one final perusal. If, then, it still yielded nothing for me, I proposed to discard it along with some other books which had outlived their usefulness in my life. So, with notebook and pencil by my side in bed, I began casually to glance through Mrs. Atwood's book, underlining a significant passage here and there, and jotting down some brief notes on the pad.

Suddenly, and to my utter amazement, the whole enigma became crystal clear and alive. The formerly mysterious *Golden Tractate of Hermes* and *The Six Keys of Eudoxus* seemed all at once to open up to unfold their meaning. Feverishly I wrote. In effect, the greater part of *The Philosopher's Stone* got written in those two weeks of bronchitis. It is true that later I added some diagrams together with a short commentary to Vaughan's alchemical text, and a few quotations from Carl G. Jung and other authors whose works were not immediately available while I was confined to bed. But actually the main body of the book was composed there and then.

My book has been praised as a good meaningful book by some reviewers and by many readers, to judge from the mail I have received during the past thirty years. It is patently an open sesame to one level of interpretation. *The Occult Review,* now defunct, published a critical review by Archibald Cockren who took me rather severely to task for asserting that alchemical texts should be interpreted solely in terms of psychological and mystical terms. He himself, I subsequently discovered, had written a book *Alchemy Rediscovered and Restored.* Of course I immediately procured a copy. Since I was peeved by his review, I did not feel that his book had very much to offer—so I dismissed both offhand. I was about to write the editor of *The Occult Review* a scorching letter, but reason intervened so that fortunately it never got written.

The opportunity is rarely given to an author in his lifetime "to eat crow" and to enjoy it. This lot, it pleases me to say, is mine—after thirty years. Not that I would significantly change much of what I wrote then. I admitted that I had not "proceeded to the praxis" but I felt then and still do that a mystical and psychological interpretation of some alchemical texts was legitimate. There is unequivocally this aspect of the subject. Certainly Jacob Boehme and Henry Khunrath, for example, cannot be interpreted except in these terms.

Nor should one be permitted to forget some of the preliminary provisions laid down by Basil Valentine in *The Triumphant Chariot of Antimony:*

This object I pursue not only for the honour and glory of the Divine Majesty, but also in order that men may render to God implicit obedience in all things.

I have found that in this Meditation there are five principal heads, which must be diligently considered, as much are in possession of the wisdom of philosophy as by all who aspire after that wisdom which is attained in our art. The first is the invocation of God; the second, the contemplation of Nature; the third, true preparation; the fourth, the way of using; the fifth, the use and profit. He who does not carefully attend to these points will never be included among real Alchemists, or be numbered among the perfect professors of the Spagyric science. Therefore we will treat of them in their proper order as lucidly and succinctly as we can, in order that the careful and studious operator may be enabled to perform our Magistery in the right way.

It is evident then that though some alchemists did work

manually in a chemical laboratory, they were at the same time men of the highest spiritual aspirations. For them, the Stone was not only tangible evidence of successful metallic transmutation; it was accompanied by an equivalent spiritual transmutatory process.

My readers will know by now that my thinking on most of these occult subjects had been profoundly influenced by the life and work of Aleister Crowley. So far as his knowledge of alchemy went, I ought to narrate that in the winter of 1897, he had gone to Switzerland for mountain-climbing and winter sports. While there he encountered a Julian Baker, with whom he had a long conversation about alchemy. This indicates at the very least that Crowley had been widely reading on this topic as well as on mysticism. As a result of this conversation, Baker promised to introduce Crowley to a chemist in London, George Cecil Jones who might be instrumental in getting him admitted into the Hermetic Order of the Golden Dawn. There is not the least shred of evidence to indicate that Crowley, Baker or Jones had done any practical laboratory work in alchemy. In magic—yes; in alchemy, no!

Many years later, Crowley came to use alchemical symbolism to elucidate the "Mass of the Holy Ghost," the sex-magic principles of the O.T.O., principles which I re-stated in the 16th chapter of *The Tree of Life*.

To refer back to the Golden Dawn, it seems to me that there was little that was really illuminating on alchemy in its curriculum, though in other areas, particularly the magical, I feel to-day as I always have.

The Golden Dawn was essentially a Qabalistic and magical order, not an alchemical one. I do not know of any evidence pointing out that Mathers or Westcott had ever engaged in operating an alchemical laboratory. One document, bearing the imprimatur of Mathers, deals with alchemy, not from the laboratory viewpoint, but from that of ritual magic—and at best it is plain verbiage. Its mystical interpretation is best expressed in a speech made by one Adept in its classic ritual: "In the alembic of thine heart, through the athanor of affliction, seek thou the True Stone of the Wise."

To this extent, the Golden Dawn had severed its traditional ties with the parent Rosicrucian bodies of Germany and Central Europe which were patently alchemical. One has only to glance casually through *The Secret Symbols of the Rosicrucians* to realize the extent to which Alchemy was considered the predominant feature in the Rosicrucian work of that era.

I know none of its members who could at any time have thrown any ray of light on alchemy. One member, the late Capt. J. Langford Garstin wrote a couple of books, *Theurgy* and *The Secret Fire* about alchemy, but they too yield little of practical value on the subject. I have met people here and there in the past forty years who could talk about Alchemy, but I cannot say that any of them made much sense.

Events in the past few years—a Uranus cycle—have conspired to force upon me a thoroughgoing expansion or reorientation of my original point of view, so that I can now quite happliy admit that Archibald Cockren was right.

How this came about is a story in itself—typical of the way in which such things occur. Through a friend of a friend of mine, I was introduced to Mr. Albert Riedel of Salt Lake City, Utah, while he was visiting Los Angeles. At the time I was domiciled there, enjoying the sunny climate and occasionally ruminating over the inclement weather of London where I was born. It took only a few minutes to realize that I was talking to the first person I had *ever* met who *knew* what he was talking about on the subject of Alchemy. We promised to keep in touch—and we did.

This promise later eventuated in an invitation to attend a seminar on Alchemy that he was conducting at the newly instituted Paracelsus Research Society in Salt Lake City. Most of the material presented in the Seminar concerned Alchemy, Qabalah, Astrology, etc.—with which I was already theoretically familiar—though even there some radically new and stimulating viewpoints were obtained. But the *piece-de-resistance* was the laboratory work. Here I was wholly dumbfounded.

It took no more than a few minutes to help me realize how presumptuous I had been to assert dogmatically that all alchemy was psycho-spiritual. What I witnessed there, and have since repeated, has sufficed to enable me to state categorically that, in insisting solely on a mystical interpretation of alchemy, I had done a grave disservice to the ancient sages and philosophers.

When Basil Valentine said, for example, in his work on antimony: "Take the best Hungarian Antimony . . . . pulverize it as finely as possible, spread thinly on an earthenware dish (round or square) . . . . place the dish on a calcinatory furnace over a coal fire . . . " he means exactly what he says—exactly and literally. When he says a coal fire, he was not referring to the inner fire or Kundalini. It is simply ridiculous to assume he is talking in symbols which must be interpreted metaphysically, etc. Once you have followed his instructions to the letter, literally, or have been privileged to have seen this laboratory process demonstrated, then you know that "manually" is certainly not meant to be interpreted as by Mrs. Atwood in terms of mesmeric passes of the hands.

There is a more or less lengthy passage in *Praxis Spagyrica Philosophica* by Frater Albertus (Salt Lake City, 1966) which is worthy of quotation at this juncture. He wrote, in a footnote to page 77 et seq:

> Some have gone to extreme pains to duplicate the ancient implements of former alchemists. They had to be able to obtain better, or at least for sure, the same results with our modern instruments. Take the regulation of heat alone. Formerly it was an arduous task requiring an assistant to keep the temperatures under control for the various manipulations. This expense alone was one that not many of the average persons could afford. To-day we have gas, natural or artifical, electricity and other means at our disposal giving us a much greater accuracy than was possible to obtain by manual operation. Vessels are stronger and not as fragile as formerly. Pyrex and similar glass containers can take much more heat and are in less danger of breaking. Stainless steel, another of the modern marvels, does away with the old copper still that had formerly many corrosive sublimates and other by-products when natural processes were followed . . . .
>
> Last, but not least, it should be remembered that many of the essential ingredients used had to be prepared by slow and sometimes hard manual operations. The required basic substances were not always as easily available as it appears. Great distances, and the necessary time involved, made it even more difficult. There was no air parcel post. Horse drawn wagons had to bring the goods that were not immediately available (sometimes from foreign countries). No telephone calls over greater distances, spanning continents, were available to make possible the information needed at a critical point . . . . Despite all these and similar hardships they were able to accomplish what many in our days cannot do. Telephone and air travel not withstanding . . . .

Again, let me repeat, my analysis of the three alchemical texts of *The Philosopher's Stone* is worth preserving. I am proud that Llewellyn Publications has seen fit to return it to print in a new edition. I should have re-written parts of the book in order to incorporate what I have since discovered through the person and work of Frater Albertus Spagyricus, the *nom de plume* which he prefers to be known by, but I have decided to let it stand as it was first written.

It did represent the dawn of insight for me then, and it was the product of a genuine illumination, partial though it was, and outgrown it as I have to-day. As such I think it has the inherent right to continued existence in its original form. Moreover, it may prove useful to other students who have not yet discovered this point of view, which certainly is a valid one. They may be at the stage of growth I was in thirty years ago, where it could be of value. It needs merely to be supplemented by other reading of more recent vintage.

In the meantime, *The Philosopher's Stone* with these preliminary comments, should answer a wide-felt need which has called forth this new edition. I hope, being in print once more, it will bring new light and knowledge and values to present-day students who may be still groping in the dark areas of the occult towards alchemy, where a guiding hand needs to be extended.

So, to close this Introduction, I must use the ancient Rosicrucian greeting, and the close of a Golden Dawn ritual:

May what we have partaken here sustain us in our search for the Quintessence; the Stone of the Philosophers, True Wisdom and perfect Happiness, the Summum Bonum.

Valete, Fratres et Sorores.

Roseae Rubeae et Aureae Crucis.

Benedictus Dominus Deus noster qui dedit nobis hoc signum.

Israel Regardie

Studio City, California
November 1, 1968

CONTENTS

LIST OF DIAGRAMS

BOOK ONE

BOOK ONE

CHAPTER ONE

INTRODUCTION

THE word Alchemy is an Arabic term consisting of the article *al* and the noun *khemi*. We may take it that the noun refers to Egypt, whose Coptic name is Khem. The word, then, would yield the phrase "the Egyptian matter", or "that which appertains to Egypt". The hypothesis is that the Mohammedan grammarians held that the alchemical art was derived from that wisdom of the Egyptians which was the proud boast of Moses, Plato, and Pythagoras, and the source, therefore, of their illumination. If, however, we assume the word to be of Greek origin, as do some authorities, then it implies nothing more than the chemical art, the method of mingling and making infusions. Originally all that chemistry meant was the art of extracting juices from plants and herbs.

Modern scholarship still leaves unsolved the question as to whether alchemical treatises should be classified as mystical, magical, or simply primitively chemical. The most reasonable view is, in my opinion, not to place them exclusively in any one category, but to assume that all these objects at one time formed in varying proportions the preoccupation of different alchemists. Or, better still, that different alchemists became attracted to different interpretations or levels of the art. There is no doubt that by some writers alchemy was interpreted in a categorical and literal sense—that is, as a chemical means whereby the baser metals could be transformed and made precious. There is a vast body of testimony to this end, evidence which cannot be made to yield any interpretation other than a physical and chemical one. On the other hand, there are certain alchemistical philosophers to whom it would be impossible to impute any other interest than a mystical or religious one.

Alchemy is also called Hermeticism. Hermes, from the mythological standpoint, is the Egyptian God both of Wisdom and Magic—which concepts include therapeutics and physical science as then it was known. All these subjects may, therefore, claim just inclusion within the scope of the significance of the terms Alchemy and Hermetic subjects.

It cannot be doubted in any way that such writers as Robert Fludd, Henry Khunrath, and Jacob Boehme aspired to and wrote of spiritual perfection, a state or mystical condition which was represented to them by the Stone of the Philosophers. With this idea I shall deal at some length in succeeding pages. It is equally certain that the first consideration of Paracelsus, for example, was the cure of disease and the prolongation of life. At the same time his greatest achievements appear to most modern thinkers to have been his discoveries of opium, zinc, and hydrogen. We tend, therefore, to think of him as a chemist no less than we do Van Helmont, whose conception of gas ranks him as one of those rare geniuses who have increased human knowledge by a fundamentally important idea.

But another viewpoint is possible here. For alongside of the genuine researchers, the alchemists who employed a psychological or spiritual technique, or who were genuine chemists or healers, we have the scrambling throng of the uninitiated. These had utterly failed to penetrate the secret of the true doctrine on any of its several levels, and commenced working on anomalous materials which could never bring them to the desired end. These were the false alchemists derisively named the Puffers. It is not, then, from alchemy proper or legitimate alchemists, as is so often assumed, that modern chemistry derives, but actually from the erratic work of the Puffers. These spent themselves in experiments on alien substances and animal excreta condemned by the true adepts. In consequence, they never achieved the desired result—the Philosopher's Stone. But on the other hand, they were led by chance into unexpected and, for us, most useful discoveries. As an instance we may cite Künckel who isolated phosphorus, which he most certainly was not anticipating. Or Blaise de Vignère who discovered benzoic acid without being aware of it. We may also cite the salts isolated by and named after Glauber.

Historically, the literature is immense. Represented in India and the Near East, in the Greek, Roman, Byzantine, and the Arabic civilizations as well as in Hebrew writings, the entire literature runs to thousands of titles. In recent years, moreover, we have had the publication of an important Chinese text. Most treatises from the *Aesch Metzareph* of the Qabalists to Valentine's *The Chariot of Antimony*, are deliberately couched in hieratic riddles. Persecution by church, and the profanation of the secrets of power, whether real or imagined, were equally dreaded by the adepts of the art. Worse still, from the modern viewpoint, these motives and these literary techniques induced their authors to insert intentionally misleading statements, the more deeply to bewilder unworthy pretenders to their mysteries. Others, ignorant of the first principles of the art, the unscrupulous charlatans whom we have seen were called Puffers, and many another quack, taking advantage of the general credulity and superstition prevailing at these times, issued utterly meaningless and nonsensical works pretending to reveal the working of the alchemical art.

With these latter I am obviously not concerned in this place. Nor, for the moment, am I interested in the purely chemical aspect of the subject, however valid such an interpretation may be. My principal concern at the moment, when Analytical Psychology and psychological methods daily prove more absorbing, is to divine whether or not there is anything concealed within these obscurities which relates to man, revealing methods of perfecting or integrating his consciousness. I believe that they do, and therefore I propose an examination of a text or two to see in what way our present views may not be enlarged.

A cursory glance at certain sections of the alchemical literature reveals the fact that the art relates to what anciently was known as Theurgy—the divine work. Its object was to afford by technical methods of meditation, reflection, magical practices and forms of interior prayer, a more rapid mode of spiritual development and an acceleration of intellectual evolution.

The alchemical and magical theories roughly amount

to this : In the course of long aeons of time, Nature has gradually evolved a complex mechanism of reaction which we call Man. Marvellous as this organism is in many ways, yet it manifests several defects. A stream cannot rise higher than its source. And without entering into the complicated and at first sight rather bewildering realm of alchemical cosmological theories, it is held that Nature has fallen from a certain divine state—from grace as it were. It may be said that man's consciousness has relegated to a subordinate place the once proud and divine universal spirit. An efficient and useful servant, it has usurped the place of its lord and master.

Because of this condition of things, it is held that by herself and unassisted Nature cannot regain her former glorified condition of equilibrium. The alchemists referred to all things within the natural realm—especially the unawakened and unenlightened man, torn perpetually by internal conflict. For man to attain something other than an intolerable state of conflict with the misery and suffering and uncertainty resulting therefrom, some other and higher means than are found in the natural state are required to transcend his constant companions of fear, inferiority, and insecurity. The alchemists assert that everything within the circle of limited and fallen Nature can only beget its kind. Hence man's own natural efforts in an intellectual direction cannot elevate him beyond his natural state and can only beget a similar kind of unregenerate, unillumined condition.   Thus the continual failure of philosophy, politics, and sectarian religion.

But there is the aphorism "Art perfects what Nature began". And, as another Alchemist has affirmed, "Our gold is produced by art, adding nothing, detracting nothing, but only eliminating superfluities." In other words, the alchemical assertion is that in man is latent an element of Wisdom which, so long as the natural state of conflict and ignorance exists, remains dormant and in obscuration. "Within the material extreme of life, when it is purified, the Seed of the Spirit is at last found." The entire object of art is the uncovering of the inner faculty of insight and wisdom, the "essence of mind which is intrinsically pure", and the removal of the veils intervening between the mind and dividing it from its hidden divine root.

Existence and the ordinary turmoil of life, the struggle and the confusion which sooner or later binds consciousness by manifold links to an unevolved infantile and emotional attitude towards life, create anxiety and deep-seated fears. We entertain fear for the morrow and in the face of the unexpected. Fear and anxiety give rise in early life to automatisms and compulsive behaviour, to what might be called a shrinkage of the sphere of consciousness. It sets up an involuntary habitual contraction of the ego instead of a full-hearted easy acceptance of whatever may come in life, be it joy or sorrow, pain or pleasure. Continued sufficiently long, this attitude develops into mental rigidity, into a closed and crystallized conscious outlook, complacent and narrow, in which all further growth is impossible. Apart from this, many people become fixed and hidebound for quite other reasons—becoming over-attached to traditional and unoriginal modes of thinking and feeling. The result is that all spontaneity of intellect and feeling is thoroughly eliminated from the realm of possibility. It is a sacrifice which entails the death of all that is creative within. The individual becomes enclosed within an iron cage of his own construction—forged through fear of life. From this, there seems no escape. No doubt consciousness becomes developed to a very high degree, to the point where it becomes clear, inventive, and trenchant. It becomes so, however, at the expense of life itself. Such a development is at the expense of flexibility and elasticity. Its cost is the loss of all that the underlying and dynamic unconscious aspect of the psyche implies—warmth, depth of feeling, inspiration, and ease of life and living. Too great a price to be paid.

Now, it is with this rigidity of consciousness, with this inflexible crystallized condition of mind, that Alchemy, like modern Psychotherapy, proposes to deal, and, moreover, to eradicate. Psychotherapy, according to one popular writer, is a means of obtaining self-knowledge through breaking down the shell of fantasy in which the ordinary person is confined. Analysis is sometimes defined as a process the object of which is to enhance consciousness. It proceeds

B

by making conscious those unconscious elements in the instinctual and morally compulsive life which experience demonstrates to be in conflict with or untrue to reality. The crystallization of the field of consciousness, with its consequent narrowing of the possibilities of experience, produces a species of living death. The alchemists proposed to kill death. Their object, by the psychological method of interpretation, was to disintegrate this inflexible rigidity of mind. This process they call the dissolution or putrefaction. Consciousness is broken down into its component parts. From this apparently amorphous and homogeneous resultant, it was their intention to reassemble the fundamental elements of consciousness on an entirely new and healthy basis. It was proposed to establish another foundation altogether, one capable of functioning in a completely regal and spiritual way. So that the divine root which, according to their theory, had become occultated and subordinated by the presumption of man's ego, is able to manifest through a mentality which is free from the defects which characterize the average intelligence. Consciousness is to be vivified utterly and is not separated from the Unconscious by a sharp and unnatural cleavage or partition from the other levels of the psyche. Thus the contents of the one part, by a reversal of values and functions, have full access of entry into the other, and vice versa.

Like modern psychological methods the alchemical formulae have as their goal the creation of a whole man, of integrity. What the psychotherapist proposes is freedom from the nervous and defensive automatisms that render men slaves of impulse and emotion, the automatism of the drunkard, for example, the drug addict, the kleptomaniac, the chronic waverer, the choleric, the coward. I make but little mention of the normal habits and automatisms of the so-called average man, though the neurotic expressions are but slight exaggerations of them. One of the reasons why psychotherapy is so difficult for the layman to grasp is that few people are aware of the preponderance of such automatic reactions in all ordinary human conduct.

Not only does Alchemy envisage an individual whose several constituents of consciousness are united, but with the characteristic thoroughness of all occult or magical methods it proceeds a stage further. It aspires towards the development of an integrated and free man who is illumined. It is here that Alchemy parts company with orthodox Psychology. Its technique envisages a religious or spiritual goal. In much the same terms as Eastern philosophy, Alchemy propounds the question, "What is it, by knowing which, we have all knowledge ?" This is the theme, allowing for variations of a minor character, pervading the entire nature of Brahmanism and Buddhism, as well as the whole of archaic philosophy and religion. The *Tractatus Aureus* avers that "All the wisdoms of the world, O Son, are comprehended in this my hidden Wisdom." It is this which gives Alchemy that peculiar attraction which always in the West it has enjoyed, regardless of whether or not its terms have been completely understood in the clear light of logical thought.

In order the better to comprehend the basic postulates of this aspect of Alchemy which are concealed in a seemingly barbarous and unintelligible terminology, I propose to provide a brief comparison of its terms with those of other systems. Here we will employ a form of the Tree of Life as understood by the Jewish Qabalists as the fundamental basis of comparison. Its capacity to refer all symbologies to a single source of reference, thus rendering them more or less intelligible by a process of classification, is the indubitable virtue of this scheme. Where it is possible I shall refer to Analytical Psychology for a more modern and readily understandable explanation. *Book One* will be commented upon precisely in that light. *The Six Keys of Eudoxus*, the second text, will be interpreted in terms of certain aspects of Magic and Animal Magnetism or Mesmerism. These two attempts at interpretation will render the third text by Vaughan more or less clear.

Since a comparatively complete exposition of the Qabalah may be found in other of my writing, it would be needlessly repetitive to go over the same ground. This diagram shows the Ten Sephiros of the Tree of Life arranged in such a way that the seven planets of the astrological scheme may be referred to them. In addition, there is another unnumbered sphere named *Daäs*, Knowledge. The Philosophy supposes this to be an entirely new principle latent within consciousness, developing or externalizing itself as and when man acquires complete and full self-consciousness. With this principle I shall not deal for the moment, though its mention was important, since it refers to an end result. It is a final goal of the system, the purified and integrated consciousness developed after the various experimental stages of the Alchemical work have been completed. The other principles, or Sephiros as they are called, I have numbered for convenience' sake. These I can now describe in terms of the usual alchemical, psychological, and other occult clichés and ideas.

For our purposes, those principles numbered 4 to 7 inclusive are more important, entering more frequently than the others into exegesis. The trinity of potencies comprising the first circle refer to that divine root of man's being which is the deepest core of the Unconscious, the "It", the "essence of mind which is intrinsically pure". It is the realization in consciousness of this root, pure potentiality, and its assimilation into the everyday thinking of man, which is the final goal of all spiritual techniques. Various faculties of consciousness, memory, will, etc., are comprised in the second and third spheres.

The principle numbered 4 is the *Ruach*, the mind, the reasoning faculties. It is referred to the element Air. I am here reminded of the archaic and primitive correspondences—geist, pneuma, ruach, breath, spirit, etc. It is consciousness itself, operating as the ruler of the body. It is also named *Tipharas*, meaning beauty and harmony and equilibrium, its symbol being the interlaced triangles. The latter indicates the union and therefore the reconciliation of two opposing elements in a single symbol. Fire is the upright triangle, and Water—the downpointing triangle. This intrinsic tendency towards reconciliation is considered implicit within the nature of consciousness. That is to say, it indicates intellectual acumen and insight into the nature of the pairs of opposites. This faculty of understanding enables it to arrive at a third and reconciling factor of poise and rhythm. Another correspondence often employed is the Sun. Since the latter is the vital centre of the solar system radiating life and heat to all about it, and without which life could not be—so at the centre of man is this rational intellectual faculty without which man is no longer man.

Inasmuch as it is the development of this particular type of consciousness which is assumed to differentiate man from and above all other creatures, elevating him above every other department of nature, it is quite often referred to as Gold, the most perfect and precious of metals. In the Alchemical texts the intellect is also one of the Three Principles, the purified Mercury ☿ defined as "philosophic,

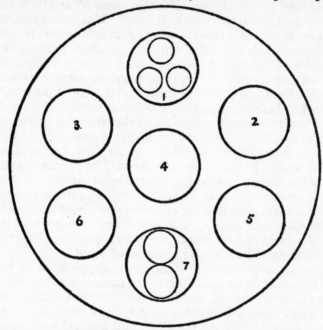

Fig. I.—THE TREE OF LIFE

fiery, vital, running, which may be mixed with all other metals and again separated from them. It is prepared in the innermost chamber of life and there it is coagulated". And again, when referred to as the Philosopher's Stone, we have this definition from *The Golden Treatise* of Hermes : "In the cavern of the metals, there is hidden the Stone that is venerable, splendid in colour, a mind sublime and an open sea." But this latter refers more accurately to the consciousness itself represented as a scintillating gem of untold price and brilliance, the redeeming, saving stone. It becomes this only after the several alchemical operations when it has been dissolved, coagulated, calcined, purified, refined, and sublimated into the newly arisen king's son, crowned with the Spirit, cloaked with the royal purple, and exalted into the treasure of the world.

The fifth principle on our chart is the emotional, feeling, and passional urge, which gives motive and direction to life. In contrast to most Western thinking, occultism sharply separates emotion as a principle from mental activity—though it is admitted that in actual practice the activities of the two do overlap each other considerably. The nature of this principle is fiery, as witness various colloquialisms and figures of speech : "the fire of thy love", "the white heat of passion", "consuming flames of passion", and "ardent desires". Alchemistically, this identifies emotion and feeling with the principle Sulphur ♣, a fiery dynamic principle, on the correct employment and application of which the entire work depends. The regimen of the Fire is the crucial and critical operation of Alchemy—even as in a lesser way it is in Psychotherapy. In certain psychological cases the awakening of a dormant or·repressed side of the patient's nature, and the union of consciousness with the *anima* or fiery emotional nature, produces integrity and wholeness and a higher synthesis of being.

The sixth principle implies form. Properly, it is the vehicular side of consciousness. Its nature is substantive. One characteristic of occult philosophy is the theorem that every state of consciousness has its own particular type of matter. We have the idea in all magical philosophy of a so-called mental body or sheath, of a mind clothed with a fluidic body of thought, grounded in a substance of extreme tenuity and subtlety. Referred to the planet Mercury (not to the alchemical principle also of that name) which implies intelligence and consciousness of a kind, its elemental attribution is Water. This latter brings out the correspondence of a fluidic plastic substance forming the etheric or astral body of the mind. The appropriate alchemical principle is Salt ⊖, the last of the triad, conceived of as an inert, heavy mineral body. Just as the alchemical Mercury refers to Consciousness, and Sulphur to emotion and feeling, so this principle of Salt refers more particularly to the sheath or vehicle in which these faculties are grounded.

After the above was written the writer glanced through Geraldine Coster's *Yoga and Western Psychology*, where the following passage occurs: "The European can readily enough grasp the idea that the physical universe is a manifestation of spirit and matter in innumerable and indissoluble combinations, because he is aware of that mysterious something called 'life' which permeates all things, but it is to him a staggering improbability that the interior processes of emotion, thought, and will possess at their own level suitable forms, forms which are substantial to the perception of those levels of experience. . . . All experiences consist of spirit-matter of varying degrees of density and the response of consciousness to this stimulus. Thus feelings and thoughts exist in space, have a shape, a rate of movement, and a period of duration."

Not only is this peculiar to all Hindu philosophy and psychology, but it underlies Hermeticism as well. To recapitulate, we have a mental body which comprises or is the seat of all the mental faculties—intelligence, emotion, will, memory, etc., together with a certain degree of plastic, fluidic, and vital substance. The whole, when it is purified and integrated, and not otherwise, forms what the Alchemists name the Philosopher's Stone.

A dual concept is contained in the seventh principle. The first half is in itself a synthetic idea. Primarily it is a concept including the three Alchemical Principles of Salt, Sulphur, and Mercury, considered as an undivided whole. It is a unit, however, only prior to the purification of art, one object of which is to differentiate them from their homogeneous base. Then, when their ideas have been assimilated to consciousness, they may sink back again into the unconscious. This principle, in its natural state, is of little value to the operator, yet without its knowledge he cannot proceed. Purified and rectified, however, it is the Stone itself, though it is then called by some other name. But within it, as said before, are the three dormant principles, for which reason it is often called Mercury alone, the other principles being considered latent and implicit. Its other names are the Quintessence, Azoth, our Water, or the

Astral Ether. It quintessentializes the four elements of
Earth, Air, Water, and Fire. It is axiomatic that any single
principle or unit is multiple when observed from a higher
level—that is, with additional insight. A multiplicity is a
unity when approached or seen from below. For example,
a table is merely a simple wooden piece of furniture to the
average person. To a more thinking type, its substance is
seen to be comprised of innumerable molecules and atoms
in varying proportions, vibrating at enormous speed so as
to give the sensory impression of solidity and hardness.
Another individual of greater insight will perceive that
what his fellow saw as a table or as a congeries of atoms,
is in reality spiritual energy polarizing itself into positive
and negative charges forming electrons, neutrons, and
protons, which circulate and move at a tremendous vibratory
rate. On its own plane, therefore, the Quintessence is a
unity synthesizing the four elements of a lower plane.
Looked at from above it is no longer simple and homogeneous
but a compound of Salt, Sulphur, and Mercury—of abstract
philosophical principles.

The Eastern equivalent of the Quintessence is *Prana*
or the life-force sustaining and permeating the body.
Since the Qabalistic and magical attribution is Air, we have
the idea of the atmosphere or oxygen concealing or being the
vehicle of a dynamizing vital principle. Here is the rationale
of certain types of Yoga breathing exercises. The breath is
the vehicle of *prana*, life, vitality, animal magnetism, which
as nervous energy transmits the commands of the Mind to the
body in much the same way as the atmosphere reflects or
transmits the heat of the Sun. So that by various kinds
of breath regulation, the practitioner of these special
modes of breathing anticipates the increase of his vitality.
As a corollary to this, such an increase is said to improve
and extend the horizon of his mind so that it comes to
embrace and recognize the spiritual principle pervading
all life and living things.

Salt, Sulphur, and Mercury are concepts synthesized
by the term Quintessence, the First Matter. This is that
which first of all must be sought out and discovered. Since
the water of the Wise, the Residual or Magical Earth, is not
physical in the ordinary sense of the word, it has been most

curiously defined and concealed. Basil Valentine, defining the nature of this First Matter, declares it to be comparable to no manifested particular whatever, and that all description fails in respect of it without the light of true experience. Sendivogius proffers that "our Water is heavenly, not wetting the hands, not of the vulgar, but almost rain water". It is heavenly, so to say, only because, like rain, it descends from the heavens above. Vaughan defines it as "a world without form, a divine animated mass of complexion like silver, neither mere power nor perfect action, but a weak virgin substance, a certain prolific Venus, the very love and seed of Nature, the mixture and moisture of heaven and earth".

Albertus Magnus states that Mercury is "a watery element, cold and moist, a permanent body, an unctuous vapour, and the spirit of the body". "O how wonderful is that Thing which has in itself all things which we seek, to which we add nothing different or extract, only in the preparation removing superfluities" is yet another panegyric to the virtues of this First Matter of the Wise.

The above will show how ambiguous these definitions are without some fairly illuminating system which may give a clarified vision of their import. It remains to be added that one's first clairvoyant view of astral matter seems to be of a white or silvery cloud, smoke, or vapour, in a state of great activity and movement. The pictures that project themselves upon it slowly unwind themselves before the mental or inner vision like a cinematograph film.

As a general concept we may more or less identify this Water of the Wise with the magician's Astral Light, and this again with the Collective Unconscious of modern psychology. It is defined by Jung in his commentary to *The Secret of the Golden Flower* as a psychic substrate common to all men alike. "It transcends all differences of culture and consciousness and does not consist merely of contents capable of becoming conscious but of latent dispositions towards identical reactions." And elsewhere he writes that "the Collective Unconscious, moreover, seems . . . something like an unceasing stream or perhaps an ocean of images, figures which drift into consciousness in our dreams or in abnormal states of mind".

We may now glance at the remaining dual concept of the seventh principle, also considered under several aspects. First of all, since the other principles have elemental correspondences, so *Malkus*, as this principle is named, is referred to the element Earth, implying solidity, firmness, and an unchanging receptacle or base in which manifest the other principles. On the other hand it is often depicted as being the sphere of the operation of the four elements of earth, air, fire, and water, whilst the other spheres are given planetary attributions.

Moreover, it may be considered as the instinctive life, the body consciousness, or the brain-mind. It corresponds with the mythological Persephone, the animal or unredeemed soul which is in exile from the promised land, lost, wandering in the wild darkness, ever in search of some abiding city. The physical body itself would seem not to be shown on this chart system, except by reference to an assumed and hypothetical subterranean world of shells. This theory implies that the physical body as such is an illusion. Not, let me hasten to add, in the false sense that it has no real existence, as some people seemed disposed to misinterpret the word. But rather, that it is not what it appears to be. The more or less permanent human form is a subtle etheric invisible body, an ideal shape or design. About and through it physical atoms, in a state of great activity and vibration, congregate and play, being attracted and repelled continuously to form by such a circulation an illusory appearance.

After a perusal of Jung's comments in *The Secret of the Golden Flower* it is difficult to gather whether, although corroborating the idea of psychic changes induced by the technique described in that book, he rejects the validity of the breath- or subtle-body hypothesis.* If this is the case, then deliberately he ignores a vast body of material which is as evidential and as strictly scientific as any body of material evidence could be. It is important to mention

---

* This was written in December 1936. The issue since that time appears to have been made considerably clearer. At this moment (March 1938) I have before me Jung's new book of Terry Lectures *Psychology and Religion*, where the following statement is made: "I have often felt tempted to advise my patients to conceive of the psyche as of a subtle body. . . ."

this inasmuch as it touches upon what the Alchemists called
their First Matter.

First of all, there are the researches and investigations
in the last century of Baron von Reichenbach. He worked
with a number of sensitives both under hypnosis and in
normal consciousness. The result of his investigations
was such as to prove beyond doubt that about each living
human being—or for that matter, around every object in
living nature—was a glow of living light, a dynamic emanation. This he called the "odic glow". Nowadays the term
for it is the aura, which is considered to be the vital emanation from this interior design- or thought-body. The hypnotic
pioneer James Braid took Reichenbach to task, attempting
to demonstrate that all of the observations which emanated
from the Baron's sensitives were due entirely and exclusively
to suggestion. Braid's attitude is really characteristic of
the whole of the extreme and one-sided scientific approach
of the last century. Fortunately it is now outworn, and we
are coming to adopt that point of view which accepts facts
rather than attempts to force facts into a predetermined
theory. The fact that Braid duplicated all Reichenbach's
results by deliberately rejecting or suggesting them to his
hypnotized subjects is by no means a valid mode of criticism.
One might as well argue that since Messrs. Maskelyne and
Devant with their intricate apparatus and conjuring
knowledge can duplicate certain of the psychic phenomena
of the psychical research societies, therefore the phenomena
there observed and recorded are disproved and invalid.
Reichenbach approached his investigations with more or less
an open mind. So far from suggesting ideas to his subjects
and sensitives, the fact remains that quite by accident they
stumbled across the various phenomena of "odism" which he
spent the rest of his life in investigating.

Reichenbach's results have within the past couple of
decades obtained definite verification from a totally unexpected source. This time, from an individual whose
orthodox standing and integrity can hardly be questioned,
and who cannot be suspected of psychic or spiritualistic
sympathies. I refer to Dr. Kilner of St. Thomas's Hospital.
He wrote a few years ago a book entitled *The Human Atmosphere*, describing his experimental work on auras. It seems

that he had invented some screens which he stained with
dicyanin, through which he examined the atmosphere
surrounding innumerable patients of his hospital. At first
sight it could be argued that what he perceived had no
necessary connection with objective reality, being simply an
optical resultant of the employment of chemical substances
and stains. On the other hand, it had an empirical value.
By this means he was able to diagnose disease, to view the
shape and size of the aura, and to describe the state and
condition of the auras of different people in varying states
of health and sickness.

Quite apart from this, however, there is a third source
of evidence. I refer to the research done by Richet, Schrenck
Notzing, Geley, Crawford, and a host of others in connection with the séance-room phenomena, quite apart from
spiritualistic theories, and this I believe convincing and
evidential. It was found that objects could be moved
experimentally at a distance, under rigorous test conditions,
without physical contact. Materialized shapes of various
kinds would manifest in the research chamber, apparently
exuded unconsciously from the body of the medium. The
substance of these shapes received a specially coined word,
ectoplasm. There is no doubt in my mind, from a critical
examination of available material, that this ectoplasm
corresponds to an objectified form of the plastic substance
comprising the interior subtle or astral body, and which the
Alchemists named their First Matter. W. J. Crawford, after
a host of experimental work with a medium, showed that her
weight and the volume of her thighs diminished when
ectoplasm was projected in the form of a materialization.
In many instances he was able not only to view such shapes,
but to feel them and observe empirically their structure.
His description of this substance is that it is cold, heavy,
damp, or, according to varying circumstances, as hard and
rigid as metal.

Geley also described this substance. He notes that it is
variable in appearance, being sometimes vaporous, sometimes a plastic paste, sometimes a bundle of fine threads,
or a membrane with swellings or fringes, etc. It may be
white, grey, or black in colour, quite often it is seen to be
luminous, as if phosphorescent. Its visibility may wax or

wane, and to the touch it may feel soft, elastic, fibrous, or hard. It has the power of self-locomotion, and moves generally as with a slow reptilian movement, though that is not to say that it is incapable of moving with extreme rapidity. It may be said to have an inherent tendency to organization, but it is of no mechanical kind. Its propensity is to take any form or shape which may be dictated or imagined unconsciously by the medium.

This is a brief description, condensed from innumerable experiments, of the substance which exudes from the body of the medium when in a trance state, and which builds itself up into bodies, heads, amorphous shapes, rods, and levers. It is this substance also which moves objects from a distance and achieves the phenomena of telekinesis, and may also become sufficiently solid to intercept an infra-red beam of light.

I have detailed these facts as proof, quite apart from other directly experiential data of the alchemical theory, that there is such an astral or design body within the physical frame. The ancient view was that it is the medium or intermediate state between mind and body, thus establishing a continuum. And that, moreover, it is the direct vehicle of the mental and emotional faculties in the fullest sense of these terms. Finally, it is this interior psychic form which is the subject of the alchemical experiment. And it is this which, because of its appearance to clairvoyant or spiritual vision, is called The Philosopher's Stone when remoulded and perfected. In the words of Khunrath: "Our King and Lord of Hosts goes forth from the chamber of his glassy sepulchre into this mundane sphere in his glorified body, regenerate and in perfection perfected, as a shining carbuncle, most temperate in splendour, and whose parts, most subtle and most pure, are inseparably blent together in the harmonious rest of union into one."

CHAPTER TWO

The Golden Treatise[1] *of Hermes Trismegistus, concerning the Physical Secret of the Philosopher's Stone.*

In Seven Sections

SECTION FIRST

1. Even thus saith Hermes : Through long years, I have not ceased to experiment, neither have I spared any labour of mind ; and this science and art I have obtained by the inspiration of the living God alone, who judged fit to open them to me His servant. To those enabled by reason to judge of truth He has given power to arbitrate, but to none occasion of delinquency.

2. For myself, I had never discovered this matter to any one, had it not been from fear of the day of judgment, and the perdition of my soul, if I concealed it. It is a debt which I am desirous to discharge to the faithful, as the Author of our faith did deign to bestow it upon me.

3. Understand ye then, O sons of Wisdom, that the knowledge of the four elements of the ancient philosophers was not corporally or imprudently sought after, which are through patience to be discovered according to their causes and their occult operation. For their operation is occult, since nothing is done except it be compounded, and because it is not perfected unless the colours be thoroughly passed and accomplished.

---

[1] The Golden Treatise, says Arthur Edward Waite in his work *The Secret Tradition in Alchemy*, first appeared at Leipzig in 1600 under the editorship of Dr. Guecias, and again in 1610. An English version was included by William Salmon in his *Medicina Practica*. Waite asserts that there is not only no Greek original but as a Latin text it is a late production. He also says Mrs. Atwood's version which is our text differs from Salmon's.

(NOTE.—The numbering of the verses does not exist in the former texts. This is simply my own inclusion, adopted for convenience' sake.—I.R:)

4. Know then, that the division that was made upon the Water, by the ancient philosophers, separates it into four substances, one to two, and three to one, the one third part of which is colour, that is to say—a coagulating moisture; but the two third waters are the Weights of the Wise.

5. Take of the humidity an ounce and a half, and of the Meridian Redness, that is the soul of gold, a fourth part, that is to say, half an ounce of the citrine Seyre, in like manner, half an ounce; of the Auripigment, half—which are eight—that is three ounces; and know ye that the vine of the wise is drawn forth in three, and the wine thereof is perfected in thirty.

6. Understand the operation, therefore, decoction lessens the matter, but the tincture augments it; because Luna after fifteen days is diminished; and in the third, she is augmented. This is the beginning and the end.

7. Behold, I have declared that which had been concealed, since the work is both with you and about you; taking what is within and fixed, thou canst have it either in earth or sea.

8. Keep, therefore, thy Argent vive, which is prepared in the innermost chamber in which it is coagulated; for that is Mercury which is spoken of concerning the residual earth.

9. He therefore, who now hears my words, let him search into them; I have discovered all things that were before hidden concerning this knowledge, and disclosed the greatest of all secrets.

10. Know ye, therefore, Enquirers into the rumour, and Children of Wisdom, that the vulture standing upon the mountain crieth out with a loud voice, I am the White of the Black, and the Red of the White and the Citrine of the Red; and I speak the very truth.

11. And know that the chief principle of the art is the Crow, which in the blackness of the night and clearness of the day, flies without wings. From the bitterness existing in the throat, the tincture is taken, the red goes forth from his body, and from his back is taken a pure water.

12. Understand, therefore, and accept this gift of God. In the caverns of the metals there is hidden the Stone that is venerable, splendid in colour, a mind sublime, and an open sea. Behold I have declared it unto thee; give thanks to God,

who hath taught you this knowledge; for He loves the grateful.

13. Put the matter into a moist fire, therefore, and cause it to boil, in order that its heat may be augmented, which destroys the siccity of the incombustible nature, until the radix may appear ; then extract the redness and the light part, till the third part remains.

14. Sons of the Sages ! For this reason are philosophers said to be envious; not that they grudge the truth to religious or just men, or to the wise ; but to the ignorant and vicious, who are without self-control and benevolence, lest they should be made powerful in evil for the perpetration of sinful things ; and in consequence philosophers are made accountable to God. Evil men are unworthy of wisdom.

15. Know that this matter I call the Stone ; but it is also named the feminine of magnesia, or the hen, or the white spittle, or the volatile milk, the incombustible ash, in order that it may be hidden from the inept and ignorant, who are deficient in goodness and self-control ; which I have nevertheless signified to the wise by one only epithet, viz. the Philosopher's Stone. Include, therefore, and conserve in that sea, the fire, and the heavenly Flyer, to the latest moment of his exit. But I adjure you all, Sons of philosophy, by our Benefactor who gives to you the ornament of His grace, that to no fatuous, ignorant, or inept person ye open this Stone.

16. I have received nothing from any, to whom I have not returned that which he had given me, nor have I failed to honour and highly respect Him.

17. This, O son, is the concealed Stone of many colours ; which is born in one colour; know this and conceal it. By this, the Almighty favouring, the greatest diseases are escaped, and every sorrow, distress, and evil and hurtful thing is made to depart. It leads from darkness into light, from this desert wilderness to a secure habitation, and from poverty and straights, to a free and ample fortune.

SECTION SECOND

1. My Son, before all things I admonish thee to fear God, in whom is the strength of thy undertaking ; and the

bond of each separated element. My Son, whatsoever thou hearest, consider it rationally. For I hold thee not to be a fool. Lay hold, therefore, of my instructions and meditate upon them, and so let thy heart be fitted, as if thou wast thyself the author of that which I now teach. If thou appliest cold to any nature that is hot, it will hurt it : in like manner, he who is rational shuts himself within from the threshold of ignorance ; lest supinely he should be deceived.

2. Take the flying volatile and drown it flying, and divide and separate it from its rust, which yet holds it in death ; draw it forth, and repel it from itself, that it may live and answer thee, not by flying away into the regions above, but by truly forbearing to fly. For if thou shalt deliver it out of its straitness, after this imprisonment, and in the days known to thee shalt by reason have ruled it, then will it become a suitable companion unto thee, and by it thou wilt become to be a conquering lord, with it adorned.

3. Extract from the ray its shadow and impurity by which the clouds hang over it, defile and keep away the light ; since by means of its constriction and fiery redness, it is burned. Take, my son, this redness, corrupted with the water, which is as a live coal holding the fire, which if thou shalt withdraw so often until the redness is made pure, then it will associate with thee, by whom it was cherished, and in whom it rests.

4. Return then, O my son, the extinct coal to the water for thirty days, as I shall note to thee ; and, henceforth, thou art a crowned king, resting over the fountain as known to thee, and drawing from thence the Auripigment dry, without moisture. And now I have made glad the heart of the hearers, and the eyes looking unto thee in hope of that which thou possessest.

5. Observe, then, that the water was first in the air, then in the earth ; restore thou it, also, to the superiors by its proper windings, and alter skillfully before collecting ; then to its former red spirit let it be carefully conjoined.

6. Know, my son, that the fatness of our earth is sulphur, the auripigment, siretz, and colcothar, which are also sulphur; of which auripigments, sulphurs, and such-like,

C

some are more vile than others, in which there is a diversity ;
of which kind also is the fat of glewy matters, such as are
hair, nails, hoofs, and sulphur itself, and of the brain, which
too is auripigment ; of the like kind also are the lion's, and
cat's claws, which is siretz ; the fat of white bodies, and the
fat of the two oriental quicksilvers, which hunt the sulphurs
and contain the bodies.

7. I say, moreover, that this sulphur doth tinge and
fix, and is the connection of the tinctures ; oils also tinge,
they fly away, which in the body are contained, which is
a conjunction of fugitives with sulphurs and albuminous
bodies, which hold also and detain the fugitive Ens.

8. The disposition sought after by the philosophers,
O son, is but one in our egg ; but this in the hen's egg can,
by no means, be found. But lest so much of the Divine
Wisdom as is in a hen's egg should be extinguished, its
composition is from the four elements, adapted and composed.

9. Know, my son, that in the hen's egg is the greatest
proximity and relationship in nature ; for in it there is a
spirituality and conjunction of elements, and an earth which
is golden in its tincture.

10. The son, enquiring of Hermes, saith—The sulphurs
which are fit for our work, whether are they celestial or
terrestrial ? And he answers, certain of them are celestial,
and some are terrestrial.

11. The Son—Father, I imagine the heart in the
superiors to be heaven, and in the inferiors earth. But
saith Hermes—it is not so ; the masculine truly is the heaven
of the feminine, and the feminine is the earth of the masculine.

12. The Son—Father, which of these is more worthy
than the other, to be the heaven or to be the earth ? He
replies—Each needs the other ; for the precepts demand a
medium. As if thou should say that a wise man governs all
mankind, because every nature delights in Society of its
own kind, and so we find it to be in the Life of Wisdom where
Equals are conjoined. But what, rejoins the son, is the
mean betwixt them ? To whom Hermes replies—In every
nature there are three from two, first the needful water,
then the oily tincture, and lastly the faeces or earth which
remains below.

13. But a Dragon inhabits all these and are his habitation ; and the blackness is in them, and by it he ascends into the air. But, whilst the fume remains in them, they are not immortal. Take away therefore the vapour from the water, and the blackness from the oily tincture, and death from the faeces ; and by dissolution thou shalt achieve a triumphant reward, even that in and by which the possessors live.

14. Know, my son, that the temperate unguent, which is fire, is the medium between the faeces and the water, and is the Perscrutinator of the water. For the unguents are called sulphurs, because between fire and oil and the sulphurs there is a very close propinquity, even as so the fire burns, so does the sulphur also.

15. All the wisdoms of the world, O son, are comprehended in this my hidden Wisdom, and the learning of the Arts consists in discovering these wonderful hidden elements beneath which it hides completed. It behoves him, therefore, who would be introduced to this our hidden Wisdom, to free himself from the vice of arrogance ; and to be just and good, and of a profound reason, ready at hand to help mankind, of a serene countenance, to be courteous, diligent to save, and be himself a guardian of the secrets of philosophy open to him.

16. And this know, that except one understandeth how to mortify to induce generation, to vivify the Spirit, to cleanse and introduce Light, until they fight with each other and grow white and freed from their defilements, as blackness and darkness, he knoweth nothing, nor can he perform anything ; but if he knoweth this, he will be of great dignity, so that the kings shall reverence him. These secrets, son, it behoves us to guard and conceal from the wicked and foolish world.

17. Understand also, that, our Stone is from many things and of various colours, and composed from four elements, which we ought to divide and dissever in pieces, and segregate in the limbs ; and mortifying the same by its proper nature, which is also in it, to preserve the water and fire dwelling therein, which is from the four elements and in their waters, to contain its water ; this, however, is not water in its true form, but fire, containing in a

pure vessel the ascending waters, lest the spirits should fly away from the bodies ; for, by this means, they are made tinging and fixed.

18. O blessed watery pontic form, that dissolvest the elements ! Now it behoves us, with this watery soul, in order to possess ourselves of the sulphurous Form, to mingle the same with our Acetum. For when, by the power of the water, the composition is dissolved, it is the key of the restoration ; then darkness and death fly away from them, and Wisdom proceeds.

SECTION THIRD

1. Know, my son, that the philosophers bind up their matter with a strong chain, that it may contend with the Fire ; because the spirits in the washed bodies desire to dwell therein and rejoice in them. And when these spirits are united to them, they vivify them, and inhabit them, and the bodies hold them, nor are they separated any more from them.

2. Then the dead elements are revived, the compounded bodies tinge and are altered, and operate wonderful works which are permanent, as saith the philosopher.

3. O permanent watery Form, creatrix of the regal elements ! who, having united to thy brethren and by a moderate regimen obtained the tincture, findest rest.

4. Our most precious stone cast forth upon the dunghill, being most dear is made altogether vile. Therefore it behoves us to both mortify two Argent vives together, and to venerate the Argent vive of Auripigment, and the oriental Argent vive of Magnesia.

5. But when we marry the crowned king to our red daughter, and in a gentle fire, not hurtful, she doth conceive a son, conjoined and superior, in it, and he lives by our fire. But when thou shalt send forth fire upon the foliated sulphur, the boundary of hearts doth enter in above it, let it be washed from the same, and the refined matter thereof be extracted. Then is he transformed, and his tincture by help of the fire remains red, as flesh. But our son, king-born, takes his tincture from the fire, and death even and darkness, and the waters flee away.

6. The Dragon, who watches the crevices, shuns the sunbeams, and our dead son will live ; the king comes forth from the fire and rejoices in the espousal ; the occult treasures will be laid open and the virgin's milk whitened. The son, already vivified, is become a warrior in the fire and over the tincture super-eminent. For this son is himself the treasury, even himself bearing the Philosophic Matter.

7. Approach, ye sons of Wisdom, and rejoice ; let us now rejoice together ; for the reign of death is finished and the son doth rule, and now he is invested with the red garment, and the purple is put on.

SECTION FOURTH

1. Understand ye Sons of Wisdom, the Stone declares : Protect me, and I will protect thee ; give me my own, that I may help thee.

2. My Sol and my beams are most inward and secretly in me. My own Luna, also, is my light, exceeding every other light ; and my good things are better than all other good things ; I give freely and reward the intelligent with joy and gladness, glory, riches, and delights ; and what they ask about I make to know and understand and to possess divine things.

3. Behold, that which the philosophers have concealed is written with seven letters : for Alpha follows two, viz. Yda and Liber ; and Sol, in like manner follows : nevertheless, if desirous to have dominion to guard the Art, join the son to Buba, which is Jupiter and a hidden secret.

4. Hearers, understand : and then let us use our judgment, for what I have written I have with most subtle contemplation and investigation demonstrated to you ; the whole matter I know to be one only thing. But who is he that understands the true investigation and inquires rationally into this matter ? There is not from man anything but what is like him ; nor from the ox or bullock; and if any creature conjoins with one of another species, that which is brought forth is like neither.

5. Now saith Venus : I beget light, nor is the darkness of my nature ; and if my metal were not dry all bodies would desire me, for I liquefy them and wipe away their

rust, and I extract their substance. Nothing, therefore, is better or more venerable than I and my brother being conjoined.

6. But the king, the ruler, his brethren attesting, saith : I am crowned, and I am adorned with a diadem ; I am clothed with the royal garment, and I bring joy and gladness of heart; for, being chained to the arms and breast of my mother, and to her substance, I cause my substance to keep together ; and I compose the invisible from the visible, making the occult matter to appear. And everything which the philosophers have hidden will be generated from us.

7. Hear then these words, and understand them ; keep them, and meditate thereon ; and seek for nothing more : Man is generated from the principle of Nature whose inward substance is fleshy, and not from anything else. Meditate on this letter and reject superfluities.

8. Thus saith the philosopher : Botri is made from the Citrine, which is extracted out of the Red, and from nothing else ; and if it be Citrine and nothing else know it will be thy Wisdom. Be not concerned if thou art not anxious to make extract from the Red. Behold, I have written to the point, and if ye understand I have all but opened the thing.

9. Ye sons of Wisdom ! burn then the Brazen Body with an exceeding great fire ; and it will imbue you with the grace which ye seek. And make that which is volatile so that it cannot fly from that which flies not. And that which rests upon the fire though itself a fiery flame, and that which in the heat of the boiling fire is corrupted is Cambar.

10. And know ye that the Art of this permanent water is our brass, and the colouring of its tincture and blackness is then changed into the true red.

11. I declare before God, I have spoken nothing but the truth. The destroyers are the renovators, and hence the corruption is made manifest in the matter to be renewed ; and hence the melioration will appear and each side is a signal of the Art.

SECTION FIFTH

1. My son, that which is born of the crow is the beginning of this Art. Behold, I have obscured the matter treated of

by circumlocution, depriving it of light. I have termed this dissolved, and this joined, this nearest I have termed furthest off.

2. Roast those things, therefore, and boil them in that which comes forth from the horse's belly, for seven, fourteen, or twenty-one days. Then it becomes the Dragon eating his own wings and destroying himself; this being done, let it be put in a furnace, which lute diligently, and observe that none of the spirit may escape. And know that the periods of the earth are in the water which is bound until you put the bath upon it.

3. The matter being thus melted and burned, take the brain thereof and triturate it in most sharp vinegar till it become obscured. This done, it lives in the putrefaction; the dark clouds which were in it before it died in its own body will be changed. This process being repeated, as I have described; it dies again as I said, thence it lives.

4. In the life and death thereof we work with the spirits; for as it dies by the taking away of the spirit, so it lives in the return and is revived and rejoices in them. Being arrived then at this, that which ye have been searching for is made apparent. I have even related to thee the joyful signs, that which doth fix its own body.

5. But these things, and how they attained to the knowledge of this secret, are given by our ancestors in figures and types; I have opened the riddle, and the book of knowledge is revealed; the hidden things I have uncovered and have brought together the scattered truths within their boundary, and have conjoined many various forms, even I have associated the Spirit. Take it as a gift of God.

SECTION SIXTH

1. It behoves us to give thanks to God, who bestows liberally to the wise, who delivers us from misery and poverty. Along with the fullness of his substance and his provable wonders I am about to try and humbly pray God that whilst we live we may come to Him.

2. Away then, O sons of Science, with unguents extracted

from fats, hair, verdigrease, tragacanth, and bones, which are written in the books of our fathers.

3. But concerning the ointments which contain the tincture, coagulate the fugitive and adorn the sulphurs, it behoves us to explain their disposition more at large. It is the Form of all other unguents in which is the occult and buried ungent, and of which there appears to be no preparation. It dwells in his own body, as fire in trees and stones, which by most subtle art and ingenuity it behoves us to extract without combustion.

4. And know that the Heaven is joined mediately with the Earth ; but the middle nature, which is the Water, is a Form along with the Heaven and the Earth. But the water holds of all the first place which goes forth from the Stone ; the second is gold ; but the third is our almost or medial gold which is more noble than the water with the faeces.

5. But in these are the smoke, the blackness, and the death. It behoves us, therefore, to drive away the vapour from the water, the blackness from the unguent, and death from the faeces, and this by dissolution. Which being done we have the sovereign philosophy and secret of all hidden things.

Section Seventh

1. Know ye then, O sons of Science, there are seven bodies—of which gold is the first, the most perfect, the king of them, and their head—which neither the earth can corrupt nor the fire devastate, nor the water change ; for its complexion is equalized, and its nature regulated with respect to heat, cold, and moisture ; nor is there anything in it which is superfluous, therefore the philosophers have preferred and magnified it, saying that this gold, in relation of other bodies, is as the sun amongst the stars, more splendid by his light ; and as, by the will of God, every vegetable and all the fruits of the earth are perfected through it, so gold, which is the ferment Ixir, vivifies and contains every metallic body.

2. For as dough, without a ferment, cannot be fermented, so when thou hast sublimed the body and purified it,

separating the uncleanness from the faeces, thou wilt then conjoin and mix them together, and put in them the ferment confecting the earth with the water until the Ixir ferment even as dough ferments. Think of this, meditate and see how the ferment in this case doth change the former natures to another thing ; observe, also, that how there is no ferment otherwise than from a kindred nature.

3. Observe, moreover, that the ferment whitens the confection and hinders it from combustion, and holds the tincture lest it should fly, and rejoices the bodies, and makes them intimately to be joined and to enter one into another, and this is the Key of the philosophers, and the end of their works ; and by this science bodies are meliorated and the operation of them, God assisting, is consummated.

4. But, through negligence and a false opinion in the matter, the operation is perverted, as bad leaven on the dough, or curds for cheese, and musk among aromatics.

5. The colour of the golden matter points to redness, and the nature thereof is not sweetness ; therefore we make of them Sericum, i.e. Ixir ; and of them we make the encaustic of which we have written, and with the king's seal we tinge the clay, and in that have set the colour of heaven which augments the sight of them that see it.

6. The Stone, therefore, is the most precious gold without spots—evenly tempered, which neither fire, nor air, nor water, nor earth is able to corrupt ; the Universal Ferment rectifying all things by its composition, which is of the yellow or true citrine colour.

7. The gold of the wise, concocted and well digested, with the fiery water, makes Ixir ; for the gold of the wise is more heavy than lead, which, in a temperate composition is the ferment Ixir, and, contrariwise, becomes distempered by an equal composition.

8. For the work begins from the vegetable, next from the animal, as in the egg of the hen, in which is the great support ; and our earth is gold, of all which we make seriacum, which is the ferment Ixir.

CHAPTER THREE

COMMENTARY

In selecting the psychological method to elucidate *The Golden Treatise* of Hermes, I have been guided solely by personal predilection. For the *Six Keys of Eudoxus* I have reserved the magnetic and magical scheme as more appropriate. The former treatise is peculiarly adapted to psychological treatment, yielding interesting and significant material. In fact one could almost imagine that the unknown author wrote his text with just such a viewpoint in mind. What has impelled me to analyse and interpret these texts is the hope that a deeper motive or a greater significance may be discovered for psychological practice than the mere elimination and cure of neurotic symptoms. While, therefore, we may learn nothing startling about method, Hermes has something significant and vital to teach us about the true goal and aim of psychotherapy. This is the justification for time and effort spent in elucidating these obscurities. In concluding her highly suggestive book on Alchemy, Mrs. Atwood has expressed the opinion that "the thresholds of ignorance are already overpast, and experiment is in need rather of a motive to dignify it than of practical machinery". Moreover, when we find a well-received modern writer on psychology, such as Geraldine Coster, insisting that Western psychology today is in need of a new impetus to a higher goal, then I hope it may be admitted that an examination of these intriguing texts on Alchemy will provide an impetus in the right direction.

Turning now to the opening verses of *The Golden Treatise*, what strikes us first is the preliminary demonstration of the essential religious or spiritual nature of the undertaking. It strikes a keynote of the entire treatise, raising the level of the interpretation of its subject matter considerably above the merely physical. Almost it implores the student to seek for a higher and loftier point of view than usually obtains. In her examination of the Yoga sutras of Patanjali, Geraldine Coster makes the contribution that not only does resignation to God imply a devotion to a personal deity conceived of in the conventional sense, but rather more. To resign oneself patiently to God's will, or to acknowledge as Hermes does that he obtained this knowledge by the "inspiration of the living God alone, who judged fit to open them to His servant", implies a thorough-going acceptance of the whole of life, so that there is no place for conflict. It suggests an unconditional acquiescence in life as actually it is, an acceptance of oneself with all one's faults and vices. It intimates a willingness to sacrifice all other aims to the one end, the attainment of the Philosopher's Stone.

3. The First Matter of the Alchemists is a synthesis or Quintessence of the four elements or qualities of dryness and moisture, heat and cold. Nothing can be done to perfect the Stone until this interior subtle or design body is first known and then subjected to a decomposing process so that its crystallization and inflexibility is brought to naught. The colours to be passed through refer to the fact that in all occult systems a different colour is attributed to each specific item of the magical alphabet. Usually for the elements we have black, russet or dark green for earth, blue for water, yellow for air, red for fire. But in the alchemical working another, possibly a simpler, attribution is employed. The sequence runs—first black to represent the decomposition or putrefaction of the Stone as first it is found. Then white—its first purified and refined state. This is followed by greenness which expresses immaturity and the possibility of complete spiritual growth, as witnessed by the colour displayed by Nature in Spring ; the colour of expectancy and hope. Red succeeds this, red for maturity, full growth, and ripeness ; whilst citrine or yellow, the colour of gold and of value and worth, is the final and desired resultant.

4. Here the First Matter is called Water. Elsewhere, and in other texts, it is named "A stone which is not a stone, spirit, soul and body, which if thou dissolvest, it will be dissolved ; and if thou coagulatest, it will be coagulated ; and if thou dost make it fly it will fly, for it is volatile and as clear as a tear."

Here are described the nature of the alchemists' basic material and the divisions made upon it. The four substances of the verse refer to the four elements of Earth, Air, Water and Fire. "One to two" represent the automatic division of the homogeneous magical Agent into its polarities of male and female, the two poles of positive and negative, active and passive, etc., the two opposites which pervade and characterize the whole of nature. These are the two extremes between which, in its unenlightened state, the ego constantly swings like a pendulum. It is this extreme which has to be overcome psychologically.

"Three to One" are the alchemical principles of Salt, Sulphur, and Mercury—the three modes of operation of the One Thing, the True Quintessence. This Water is comprised of intelligence—Mercury ; feeling—Sulphur ; and energy-substance—Salt.

5. This is obscurity and *vanitas vanitatis*. These further veils are deliberately employed, we are constantly assured, in order to confuse the ignorant and unworthy. The humidity possibly refers to the magical Earth, Meridian Redness is Fire, citrine Seyre is Air, and Auripigment is Water. The instruction simply names the ingredients of the Stone.

The Vine of the Wise is the perfected and purified Stone. It bears comparison with the opening verses of the 15th chapter of the Gospel of St. John :

I am the true Vine, and my Father is the husband-man. Every branch in me that beareth not fruit he taketh away ; and every branch that beareth fruit, he purgeth it, that it may bring forth more fruit. Now ye are clean through with the word which I have spoken unto you. Abide in me, and I in you. As the branch cannot bear fruit of itself, except it abide in the vine ; no more can ye, except ye abide in me. I am the vine, you are the branches. He that abideth in me, and I in him, the same bringeth forth much fruit ; for without me ye can do nothing.

The Vine yields wine for man's pleasure. But it does so only through the application of an intelligence and a skill external to itself. Itself unaided, it remains but a vine. So by the alchemical artifice of putrefaction and distillation, the crude material of the astro-mental sheath is purified, becoming, so to speak, the wine or spirit thereof. Noteworthy also, is the fact that the Vine and wine generally are sacred in mythology to Bacchus. On the Qabalistic Tree of Life he is referred to *Tipharas*, the solar centre, the source of reference of all the dying Gods who teach immortality, resurrection, and healing. The glorified and purified consciousness which is the Philosopher's Stone is likewise a *Tipharas* attribution—and often is termed the Augoeidês, the deathless solar body, the wedding garment of scripture. Thus the Stone is immortality, it is consciousness resurrected from death, gifted with divine healing.

6. The method of working is here summarily described. Luna is the celestial symbol of the Astral, the philosophical Water, and therefore of the Collective Unconscious. In every system of ancient symbolism, the Moon refers to the Soul of the World. The first part of the operation, represented by the waning of the moon, the dark fortnight, is the breaking down process—decoction, putrefaction, which dissolves the matter, and discharges all and every impurity. The second half is the bright fortnight, the waxing of the Moon—the reverse half of the "Solvé et Coagula" formula, the reconstruction, the coagulation of the volatile.

8. Argent-vive is Mercury which, naturally, is within man himself, in the innermost chamber of his being. It is the world of the psyche itself. Another definition is given by Hermes. He calls it the residual Earth ; that is Holy Earth. Here we have a reference on the Tree to the sphere of the operation of the four elements. Another name for it is the unredeemed Virgin, the animal Soul in its natural state. *Yesod* the upper half of the seventh sphere on the diagram represents the state of the first purification, of which the term Quintessence can be used. "If you have found this argent vive, which is the residuum of the philosophic earth after the purification, keep it safely, for it is worthy." Also note the encouragement that Vaughan gives, for he says : "If thou dost know the First Matter, know also for certain that thou hast discovered the Sanctuary of Nature. There is nothing between thee and her treasures but the door. That indeed must be opened."

10. On the Tree of Life there are several other *Sephiros* of which but little mention has heretofore been made. It will now be found useful to consult the chart. The uppermost three spheres called the Supernals are often classed together as a unit. As such, this triad is then governed by the attributions of the third Supernal *Binah*, which synthetically represents the Supernals. *Binah* means Understanding, and as a glyph of the Triad conceals Wisdom and the essence of the divine Light. Thus the Supernals are Spirit, the so-called Light itself, the concealed and unknown higher Self in man.

One of the astrological attributions to *Binah* is Saturn, among whose correspondences are such ideas as stability, peace, blackness, death, time, etc. Notoriously the Vulture is a bird of prey, living on corpses and refuse. Hence, it is a particular idea or a symbol that can be included within the larger abstract generalization of Saturn. The versicle we are dealing with reads, "A Vulture stands upon the mountain." Constantly recurring in all mystical literature is this theme of a mountain. The Psalmist lifted up his eyes to the hills, Moses obtained the books of the law on Horeb. Jesus ascended the mountain to deliver his sermon. It refers evidently to an illumined or heightened state of consciousness, to spiritual heights of exaltation. It is that inward divine peak when, turned inwards in meditation and prayer, the soul withdraws to its own root and source of perfection.

In addition to being that bird which preys upon deceased and putrefying things—represented in Alchemy by the corroded First Matter—the Vulture is also a maternal symbol. *Binah* has another correspondence or association, the Great Mother. She it is who gives birth to the divine newly formed Stone, after her surrogate symbol, the Vulture, that is illumination and the lapse of time, has devoured (changed) the substance of which it is formed. The Vulture in its travels flies extremely high, and is capable of wheeling about slowly, seeming often to remain poised and stationary in mid-air. It is also credited with extremely clear and penetrating vision, sensing its prey from a distance of many miles. For our purposes then it represents extraordinarily clear and penetrating insight, intuitive understanding, and the "immovable" illuminating Spirit within.

As the Supernals are conceived of as the Light, white in colour, the Vulture's speech becomes moderately clear. *Malkus*, the secondary meaning of the seventh sphere, is the residual earth and is black, whilst the Supernals, which are the highest extreme of the Tree, represent the same residual earth brought to transcendental perfection—to whiteness. "Red of the white" would convey a further ripening of that process, of bringing it ineluctably to maturity and ripeness. The citrine is the colour of gold, the perfect metal, *Tipharas*, the sphere of harmony and balance. It is neither transcendental nor terrestrial but the reconciliation of both, the child of the extremes, the integrated consciousness between, the Middle Way. The Supernals are divine wisdom and understanding, the Truth itself.

11. The Crow is the so-called bird of Hermes—the volatile astro-mental body, capable of sustained and prolonged flights of ideation and fantasy. It requires no wings ; it is Air itself.

The throat is the seat of the voice, the instrument of the expression of the mind. Speech is the *logos* of thought, giving evidence of thought. The tincture is clearly a mercurial extract, a thought-extract—it is therefore that intellectual ferment which eventually transforms consciousness. Moreover, the throat is the seat of *Daäs*, the unnumbered centre on the Tree which is made manifest in man as evolution proceeds, as self-consciousness and perfection are developed. Because of its colour, the bird refers more particularly to that aspect of the psyche which is the unredeemed animal soul *Malkus*. It is evident that Red represents Sulphur, intensity of feeling and emotion and it "cometh from him" as we ascend the Tree. "And from his back is taken a pure Water" —that is *Yesod* again, the Quintessence, the water of the Wise, "the viscous humidity made by the dissolution which radically dissolves all metals, and reduces them into their first ens, or water".

12. Again, we have definitions of the First Matter and of the Stone—a classical and oft-repeated definition particularly. The alchemists considered the discovery of the First Matter so important that although unwilling or unable to give absolutely clear indications of its nature, they were anxious constantly to throw out suggestive hints. It was their

belief that study and meditation would expand such hints into tangible ideas.

"The cavern of the metals" evidently refers to the interior depths of Man, the principles of whose external form are the metals drawn from the mineral kingdom. As such it is an excellent symbol for the Unconscious.

13. Here now we have the first instructions as to the practical nature of the hermetic work. The First Matter, which is to say the hard, inflexible condition of consciousness encased in its crystallized sheath, must be subjected to heat, and boiled. By these means the dryness and crystallizing qualities of the etheric substance are destroyed, leaving only the essential root nature of the substance, devoid of the rigid and restricting attributes imposed upon it by the natural self-willed life.

To refer yet again to Miss Coster, we find the following clue to the meaning and significance of heating and boiling :

It is the nature of the human mechanism to set or harden into fixities of habit, and this is true not only of the body but of the mind and emotions. Speaking figuratively, it is as though the mento-emotional nature tended to harden like the stuff in an old glue-pot. The material must be brought to a perfectly homogeneous fluid consistency, and the relaxation of habitual restraint is comparable to a melting process.

I am inclined to believe that this last analogy would meet with the approval of the alchemical writers themselves, though I tend to the belief that rather more is implied by the technical use of the word "fire" in our text.

An internal agent is mentioned which is the secret fire of the alchemists. It is the effect of this fire which, it is said, reduces the silver-grey substance of the astral vehicle to dark ashes, the black Saturn. Here is the central secret of the alchemical art. All the operations depend upon this caloric operation, the regimen of the Fire. Almost *ad nauseam* are we given reiteration and emphasis of this fact. Yet no single text gives a clear straightforward indication either as to its real nature or the means of its kindling. Even the symbols employed are of such a catholic and generic nature that they can be made to yield almost anything.

We determined previously that the dynamic nature of the feelings and emotions could well be symbolized by fire, particularly in view of poetic expressions and widely employed colloquialisms and local idioms. On the other hand, from a philosophical point of view, we could equally argue that because of its penetrating, incisive and illuminating quality the intellect might be that fire so beloved of the alchemists. This would imply that they were thinkers and philosophers almost after the fashion of the Schoolmen, delighting in sophistries and intellectual quibbles. With these symbols, it is obvious, however, that we make but little real progress.

Turning for aid to the psychological realm we are confronted with a maze of symbols which some consider illuminating, whilst others in all sincerity and intellectual honesty believe to be of no final value. For example, the Freudian interpretation of the nature of the furnace, the fire, and the oven is exclusively in terms of sex. That is to say, objects such as the furnace or the oven represent the female genitalia. Heat itself is, according to Freud's manner of seeing things, sexual excitation or libido, which he defines solely in terms of sexual desire. Popular expression known to almost everyone certainly lends some degree of credence to the idea of heat as sexual desire. In his *Introductory Lectures on Psycho-Analysis*, Freud observes that :

> The kindling of fire and everything connected with this is permeated through and through with sexual symbolism, the flame always standing for the male organ, and the fireplace or the hearth for the womb of the mother.

An analysis of the alchemical text along these lines would lead us finally to the conclusion that the unknown author was indulging consciously or otherwise in a sexual phantasy. Hence a detailed analysis of it would produce nothing of any ultimate psychological or practical value other than providing us with a new set of symbols for the sexual organs and the sexual act and infantile fantasies concerning their use.

D

It is, I am quite willing to agree, a valid line of interpretation. And, in point of fact, it was along such lines as these that I proceeded when dealing with alchemy in a former work. In the 16th chapter of my *Tree of Life* I produced as symbolical of the penis and semen the ideas of the alchemical Athanor and the Blood of the Red Lion. The Curcurbite and the Gluten of the White Eagle were symbols to represent the female genitals and their secretion. But adolescent fantasies of this kind are of no deep spiritual significance. They teach us nothing with regard to the object enunciated as my principal interest. We learn nothing of practical means of integrating the human psyche, of developing its latent faculties, of elevating it to a loftier level of function and psychic action. I discard therefore without further argument the Freudian interpretation unless it be subjected to considerable modification and extension.

If we do accept the furnace as being a female symbol, then, instead of halting desperately here, we must proceed along an extended association track to discover other valid meanings and significations for such ideas. The sexual correspondence is a perfectly valid objective association. It is accurate as far as it goes. But its meaning is considerably enhanced if we transfer it to the subjective level—that is if we ascertain what is the symbolic meaning, either to the dream faculty or the active imagination, of women and their sexual organs. So far as man is concerned, women represent three things : *First*, their primary reaction to life is an emotional one ; it is always expressed in terms of feeling, love, and emotion. *Second*, they represent sexually an object of gratification. *Third*, as the mother they represent the source of human life. Thus we have several correspondences for the alchemical furnace and the fire it generates. It represents something whose action is generative, from which pleasure may be derived, and which has a definite association with the emotional faculties. It may be contended, therefore, that if we associate the furnace with the Unconscious we have a valid and reliable correspondence. The female symbol is the furnace-Unconscious, whilst the masculine one is the fire-libido. In my opinion a consideration of the text along broader lines such as these will yield infinitely more meaning and practical information than if we adhered to what is in reality an adolescent fixed and unscientific code of symbol attribution.

Dr. Jung, who differs very considerably from Freud's rather narrow sexual interpretations, has something to say on this question of fire in his Commentary to *The Secret of the Golden Flower*. Referring to the Chinese text, he remarks that

> These verses contain a sort of alchemistic instruction as to a method or way of creating the "diamond body", which also appears in our text. "Heating" is necessary ; that is, there must be a heightening of consciousness in order that the dwelling-place of the spirit can be "illuminated". But not only consciousness, life itself must be heightened. The union of these two produces "conscious life". According to the *Hui Ming Ching*, the ancient sages knew how to bridge the gap between consciousness and life because they cultivated both. In this way the immortal body is "melted out" and in this way "the great Tao is completed".

15. Here follow further instructions on the Stone, each one, by meditation, revealing some further point in clarification of the issue. Again we have technical references to a method to be pursued. The Heavenly Flyer is consciousness, the human soul so-called. The Fire is the internal re-creative agent, suggesting an intensity of feeling and emotion. On the other hand, the action of a keen and penetrating intellect, which burns up dross and confused thinking, may well be likened to Fire.

Quite valid at this juncture are the psychological correspondences, and they follow the same routine as we followed above. Generally speaking, free association will produce the Mother as an association of Sea. The Mother is the source and root from which we have come ; that which has given us birth. Transferring the objective symbol to the purely subjective level, the Mother as an idea is related to the Unconscious. It is axiomatic that consciousness is a more or less recent development in the long history of man, and the Unconscious is its source and antecedent. Consciousness is born from and issues out of the dark creative fertile depths of the Unconscious. The Unconscious, wrote Jung, is always there beforehand as a potential system of psychic functioning handed down by generations of men. Consciousness, however, is a late-born descendant of the unconscious psyche. It would certainly show perversity if we tried to explain the lives of our ancestors in terms of their late descendants ; and it is just as erroneous and stupid to regard the unconscious as a derivative of consciousness. We are much nearer the truth if we put it the other way round.

In this event, we must enlarge the psychological idea of the Unconscious very considerably. We have identified this Collective Unconscious with what in occultism is called the *Anima Mundi*. But even in magical literature this latter concept is conceived to have two aspects or poles, if so we may speak. To explain their nature, we may be obliged to use in addition to the word Unconscious another term not in general acceptance, the Superconscious. This includes all the finer spiritual aspirations, inner faculties of discrimination and innate wisdom and love. Both of these principle concepts have become united in the general term, the Unconscious. So long as we understand this, no harm may come. But it would be erroneous to suppose literally that consciousness has issued from the lower levels of the *Anima Mundi*. This latter is itself a derivative—so runs magical philosophy—of the higher more divine level, corresponding to the supernal triad of Spirit and Wisdom and Understanding.

But before consciousness can attain to the Supernals, it must have passed through Avernus. And this is the implication of the text. Consciousness and feeling together must, by no matter what means, be immersed in the fructifying sea of the Unconscious. Naturally, this would appear at first as a destructive process. For as Jung has so concisely expressed it :

> Danger arises whenever the narrowly delimited but intensely clear individual consciousness meets the immense expansion of the Collective Unconscious, because the latter has a definitely disintegrating effect on consciousness.

This species of disintegration, of conscious schizophrenia, is precisely what the alchemists wish to produce as their first step. For one thing, if the process is accomplished deliberately and consciously, the larger part of the danger is eliminated. In fact to do so implies an understanding of the mechanism of the unconscious. And such a knowledge, psychotherapists inform us, confers freedom from unconscious automatisms, from compulsive domination of consciousness by repressed material stored in the Unconscious, and also from the dangers of any such lack of insight and discrimination.

Their practical experience has taught them, the alchemists aver, that if the immersion of the heavenly flyer in the Sea where lies latent the internal fire be repeated sufficiently often, then instead of destruction being effected, the nascent spirit stirs to renewed activity. The German poet Holderlin has written : "Danger itself fosters the rescuing power."

And moreover, to quote Jung once more :

What we observe here is a fundamental law of life— *enantiodromia*—the reversal into the opposite ; and this it is that makes possible the reunion of the warring halves of the personality, and thereby brings the civil war to an end.

The result of this renewal of life is a second birth. For the elements of consciousness, or the human soul and its vehicle, are reassembled spontaneously upon an entirely new and higher pattern. This new consciousness is the result of the *union* of the several constituents of consciousness, or levels of awareness. Its major characteristic is the absence of any hard-and-fast barrier or partition which consciousness has erected before the portals of the Unconscious. A harmony is established between the human soul and infinite life without. The result is the ability of the natural vital spirit to flow freely into all the parts and levels of the whole consciousness, producing health and true happiness and integrity.

Alchemists frequently quote Francis Bacon with regard to this law of *enantiodromia,* as follows :

And if any skilful minister shall apply force to nature ; and, by design, torture and vex it in order to its annihilation, it, on the contrary, being brought to this strange necessity, changes and transforms itself into a strange variety of shapes and appearances ; for nothing but the power of the Creator can annihilate it or truly destroy ; so that, at length, running through the whole circle of transformation and completing its period, it in some degree restores itself, if the force be continued.

It is the spontaneous reversal of the spiritual life, the restoration of itself after continuous and persistent attempts to dissolve the frame and groundwork of the soul which the alchemists believed to occur, and claimed, furthermore, to have achieved.

17. The perfected inner body restored spontaneously to itself by its own inherent dynamic power, glows and scintillates outwardly with an inward light like a diamond or other very precious jewel. It is interesting here to quote Aleister Crowley's description of the aura, which is the glorified inner body together with its own dynamic emanation :

The Aura should be clean-cut, resilient, radiant, iridescent, brilliant, glittering. "A Soap bubble of razor-steel, streaming with light from within", is my first attempt at description ; and it is not bad, despite its incongruities.

It is the opinion of the Zürich school that the development of this inner or diamond body is the automatic adjustment on the part of the psyche itself in its preparation for death. Jung declared that such a development is "psychologically symbolical of an attitude which is invulnerable to emotional entanglements and violent upheavals ; in a word they symbolize a consciousness freed from the world. I have reasons for believing that this is a natural preparation for death, and sets in after middle life. Death is psychologically just as important as birth and, like this, is an integral part of life". And a little further on, the same psychological exponent refers to the "psychic spirit-body ('subtle body') which ensures the continuity of the detached consciousness".

As our text puts it, with regard to this newly found but still highly concealed stone, "it leads from darkness into light, from this desert wilderness to a secure habitation, and from poverty and straits to a free and simple fortune".

This is that celebrated Elixir of Life which, freed from every restriction on the part of an inelastic, confused, and unseeing mentality, is said to prolong life—though we need not necessarily interpret this in a wholly physical sense. It is a truism in certain philosophies that man is not immortal though his essence is. His immortality as an individual conscious entity is a condition of things that requires achievement through his own unaided and unfailing effort.

Certain comparative philosophical views are worthy here of consideration. Notably, the Buddhist idea as contrasted with typical Western ideas. As is more or less well known, all schools of Buddhism hold that man has no individual ego or permanent unit of consciousness which is capable of surviving death, as is maintained both by Hindu philosophers and those of the West. Whilst in Buddhism the idea of transmigration or reincarnation is held, the rationale or *modus operandi* departs considerably from the usually held idea that it is the immortal ego which incarnates again and again. It is the Buddhist claim that man is comprised of various bundles or aggregates of attributes and qualities. Their view, moreover, is that man is a combination of several consciousnesses strung together by natural law to form an apparent unit. So far as his ego-sense is concerned, their psychology holds it to be a false perception. It is a convenient expression to speak of the ego just as commonly we still refer to the rising and setting of the sun. Such a view is directly attributable to taking appearances on their face value and ignoring the true nature of reality. It is precisely this ego-sense, false and illusory, which impedes the perception of the true nature of reality, of the universe as it is in and for itself. From such a point of view it follows that the goal to be sought—since this false ego-sense is responsible for an imperfect view of life and thus responsible for suffering, mental conflict and psychic torture—is the dissolution of that obstinate and persistent falsity. This accomplished by various means, the aggregate, which is called man, sinks into the Void. Buddhism considers the Void most certainly not as a negative conception of nothingness, but rather as analogous to transcendental divinity, the Clear Light, or absolute Consciousness.

In the West, however, ignorant though we may be of the loftier flights of the philosophic and spiritual perception indubitably enjoyed by the protagonists of the Mahayana *Bodhi*, our point of view is fundamentally different. It is the Occidental view that the ego has some value for us in that we are individual human beings obliged by our destiny to deal with a very practical world. Therefore the egocentric concept has been preserved despite all arguments and efforts to the contrary. This is not to say that our philosophers fail to realize the defects and the inadequacies and the occasional lapses of the ego itself. On the contrary this is clearly recognized. The Western religious and philosophic ideal seems to be the enlightenment of the mind by God or the Absolute or the Universal Spirit removing the tarnish from the bright mirror of the mind. It tends to nullify the false accretions which a worldly civilization builds around the ego, without in any wise wishing to destroy the ego itself. The ego as a separate practical psychic entity they seek to preserve in its own right that it may consciously manifest to the world the divine consciousness which informs it. "Life and yet more life" is the prevalent ideal here. And illumination which sanctifies life through a purified and clarified consciousness seems to be, summarily speaking, the central pivot of its system—god and man conjoined in a single being.

Alchemy, in Europe, has acquired a singularly Occidental flavour, and this too is pretty much the Alchemical ideal. To manifest and use the Stone of the Wise for the further glory of God is that ideal. Its virtue over and above other Western systems is that it provides a practical scheme to this end. A glorified body with a purified spirit and soul elevated to the heights of spiritual kingship—a glorified inner pneumatic body used by a regenerated soul—is the attainment it holds up. No final dissolution does it countenance, or an absorption at the expense of the ego. This, in its eyes, would imply the extinction of the individual.

At the outset of the second section Hermes again emphasizes the essentially spiritual attitude required of him who would undertake this divine work. Were Alchemy a mere torturing and vexing of material metals, such a stand would be absurd. And, moreover, our author shows by what means the knowledge of the divine art may be obtained. For whilst all the alchemists urge that nothing can be known of the spagyric art save by the grace of God, yet Hermes states the entire process is a rational one and urges constant reflection and meditation on rational principles. This being so, the art must be accessible to rational inquiry if conducted in the right way and if persisted in so as to penetrate the convention of the apparently arbitrary use of obscurities. Meditation above all must lead to the solution of the great problem. Together with diligent study of his protracted instructions, aided by sincerity, devotion and a complete acceptance of life and human nature, meditation will lead far if conducted with or motivated by a true spiritual motive. Hermes urges that reflection on the matter is of tremendous importance and persisted in will impart the vital clues. For, says he, consider the text as though you, the reader, had written it. In such a way, one may identify oneself with the motive of the writer and sense or intuit his purpose. Consider the writer's motive for the employment of the various phrases and conventionalities of expression. Probe into the significance of his various instructions and "so let thy heart be fitted" for the truth.

2. Having premised this much, at once the venerable adept dives into the obscure deeps of alchemical intricacy. The "rust" of the verse is, evidently, the crippling superficial world-view of the individual, which corrupts and corrodes consciousness and its experience of life. Infantility, compulsive behaviour, adherence to adolescent expression both of feeling and thinking—these are the traits which interfere with the free growth and expression of the psyche. Not only so, but if persisted in, and if they become chronic or severe or intense, we have the production of psychosis, true schizophrenia, and other forms of insanity—rusts which eat up the metal of consciousness and involuntarily disintegrate the ego itself.

Therefore we are to take consciousness, which in view of the airy volatile nature of the mind is named by the text as the Flying Volatile, and drown it flying. The curious use of the last phrase is most intriguing. It seems to indicate the specific nature of the technique employed. That is to say consciousness is to be drowned by its own activity—whilst it flies. It would point to the immersion of consciousness in the Sea—"drowning" points in that direction—by its own intellectual and critical activity. Analytical therapy would most certainly correspond to such an activity. Certain forms of meditation likewise function in much the same way. Often, during the course of analysis, the patient becomes quite unsettled and disturbed. The analytical process consists of an impartial critical examination of the memory, fantasy, feeling and the other contents of consciousness in order to divine their origin and significance, and thus to estimate their true value. Moreover the contents of the Unconscious well up from the hidden depths and make their appearance at various stages either in dream or by direct perception and feeling. It may sometimes appear to the analysand, when he has learned a little of the art of mental relaxation and can actually loosen his emotional tension, that he is in danger of being swamped or overwhelmed by the wealth of unconscious image and ideation that arises. The entire therapeutic process is accomplished by the active use of the consciousness whose contents are being examined and changed, and whose boundaries and horizon of vision are being enlarged and enhanced. By immersing consciousness in, at first sight, the disintegrating sea of the Unconscious, it is divided from "its rust which yet holds it in death". That is, these infantile attitudes and fantasies which are so inhibiting and disturbing to consciousness are seen for what they are, and in the light of a dawning understanding and discrimination are discarded.

Mental conflict, when unconscious, as usually it is, is always inhibitory and leads to indecisive action and loss of physical and mental tone. Conflict invariably, though not inevitably, arises from a one-sided and unbalanced attitude towards life. It arises either from a stressing of conscious viewpoints at the expense of those of feeling and emotion, or vice versa. Such an attitude may lead to a sudden loss or withdrawal of libido. All our previous activities may become uninteresting, even senseless, and the goals towards which we strive lose their value.

Conscious conflict, however, has another value, quite

apart from the superficial fact that a conscious conflict can consciously be dealt with. Our text appears to encourage conflict when, however, it is cultivated deliberately and with full intent in order to hasten the cessation of its activity. Then follows a new birth and production of an integrated attitude which appertains to neither element of the conflict. What possibly is a more accurate expression is not that conflict is encouraged consciously or otherwise, but that analysis and meditation increase the perception of the presence of the conflict so that the true extent of the internecine warfare waging within is fully realized. Jung has described at some length in *Psychological Types* the phenomenon whereby the conflict between the pairs of opposites when becoming too acute to be borne, causes consciousness of them to undergo an eclipse. A third or higher reconciling point of view spontaneously comes to birth and is the outcome of surmounting or growing out of a psychic position which is untenable and unendurable.

Whilst this battle royal proceeds, every care must be taken to prevent consciousness from flying off at a tangent, an escape, a defensive operation of the self-preservation mechanism. The hysterical escape from one opposite to another, from the sea beneath into the "regions above", must be checked, the pain and torture of the conflict being accepted and endured. Then, says the text, the hysterical symptoms of escape pass away and disappear, and the flying volatile will truly forbear to fly. Patiently will it endure the appalling unsettling of itself, the threatened disintegration of its own being, with the quiet stoicism of a sage. And it does so primarily because of its full acceptance of itself and of the conflict raging within.

Fairly obvious is the result. If the analysand can endure the exposure of his inner life, the destruction of long-cherished points of view, the elimination of beloved yet loathsome symptoms and behaviour, by arriving consciously at an understanding of his own realized self, by how much is he not enriched.

The rest of the text is comparatively clear. In making conscious and assimilating with intent the wealth of content domiciled in the Unconscious, the vast inspiration, the peace and power, Consciousness itself is enhanced. And it becomes a suitable companion. The psyche thus integrated and made whole is indeed "a conquering lord, with it adorned".

3. Because of the highly specialized nature of consciousness, its exaggerated independence and self-satisfaction and the guilt sense resulting therefrom, a barrier is erected in the psyche of modern man between the several levels of consciousness. The treatise calls this barrier set up by persistent repression, "the shadow and impurity by which the clouds hang over it, defile and keep away the light". In fact, it is common evidence that many neurotics, feeling themselves cut off from their roots and thus from the vibrant stream of life about them, imagine that actually clouds do hang over them, darkening their lives. Freud calls this overshadowing cloud of self-criticism and recrimination the Super-ego. It prevents a free and adequate contact with people and things, dulls the brain, inhibiting the easy flow of life and light, the libido, from welling up from the Unconscious. The ray is, I take it, the light itself shining over and into consciousness after the latter has been separated from or has deliberately absorbed (accepted) its shadow.

It is because of the psychic inhibitions, the "constrictions" of Hermes, that consciousness becomes inflamed and feverish within the narrow boundaries to which it is confined by repression—the fiery redness. These burn the psyche, causing it to become restless and costive, unable to accept and adapt itself to life, ill-capable of functioning smoothly and easily. Repression might be an alternative word to that employed by Hermes.

The Water is the Unconscious—using the latter in its widest sense to include not only the realm of instinct and emotion but also of the highest intuition and wisdom. It is the domicile, so to say, of the libido, vital energy, the fire of life. The association of water with fire seems curious. It recalls other alchemical allusions, such as "the fire of thy water". And again, "Inwardly at its (water) heart there burns purest infernal fire." Likewise The Golden Treatise speaks of the "water, which is as a live coal holding the fire".

Invariably a neurosis is caused by repression of certain at one time conscious material. Thrust into the deepest portions of the psyche, this material remains as an autonomous unit, fed by libido, and rendered a powerful complex of ideas.

Gradually, by association, this latter extends itself. Nervous and physical symptoms of disorder, as well as psychic compulsions, owe their existence to the repressed complex refusing, as it were, to abide quietly and peacefully in the Unconscious. It becomes explosive and dangerous. And since it has become associated with other variegated ideas, innocuous in themselves and which are not necessarily to be repressed, it forces an entry into consciousness by a backdoor method. These repressions torment and constrict the psyche. Its integrity and sense of security is attacked. The therapeutic mode of release is to become aware of what in the past has happened and what is now happening to oneself, and no longer to repress what really must be expressed in daily life. The unconscious material, set free and assimilated rationally into consciousness, is relieved of its explosive tendency, and thereby becomes, so to speak, purified. It no longer seeks a forcible exit.

To face the neurosis or repression frankly, and thus to accept it, robs it of its terror, lifting it out of the unconscious psyche where it became charged with psychic energy emerging continuously from the very deepest parts of the self. Released from the unconscious where it had obtained vitality and life, the inhibited material no more acts on consciousness in a compulsive way. No longer does it seek vengeful expression outside its normal and proper sphere. That is to say, the dynamic stimulus of the Unconscious is withdrawn from the inhibitions and fiery redness, the neurotic symptoms or distressing qualities of the ego, and the "redness is made pure". The symptoms subside, or else resume their usual function in the psychic economy. They "associate with thee by whom it was cherished, and in whom it rests".

The rationale of the process is purification by understanding. To understand the Unconscious is at once to be freed from its domination.

4. The symptoms having subsided by the pursuit of this technique—by the assimilation of Unconscious material—the psyche having regained its integrity, and strengthened by the vast accretion of libido brought up by the released material, is definitely enriched. It is freed to the point where Hermes is justified in speaking of it as a crowned king. It

rests over an inexhaustible fountain of life, for such is the nature of the Unconscious and the life-force which ever flows through it.

5. Here is an injunction with regard to the component principles of our Philosophic Water—the Unconscious. The elements themselves require stimulation and purification before being reconstructed in the proposed new and per-fected form. In ancient magical systems of initiation the candidate had to pass through so-called elemental initiations. The spirits of the element were invoked in four specific rites, each one relating to a different element. And the impact of their power upon the psyche of the candidate purified him, awakening within the psychic realm a dormant faculty corresponding to the nature of the element. The true power of the element is also imparted to the interior astral form which is being consolidated by the ceremonial system. But I shall deal more fully with the ceremonial aspect in a later chapter.

"Convert the elements," says Arnold of Villa Nova, "and you shall have what you desire." And Mrs. Atwood elaborates by adding: "Separate matter into its essential relationships and join them together in harmonious pro-portion." Whilst Jung writes in *The Secret of the Golden Flower*:

> Without doubt, also, the question of making the opposites conscious (conversion) means reunion with the laws of life represented in the unconscious or, expressed in Chinese terms, the bringing about of *Tao* (the conscious way of union).

The phrase, "restore thou it, also, to the superiors by its proper windings", is, I believe, a significant phrase. For this reason. The Qabalistic Tree of Life, which we have decided to use as our means of reference, may be looked at from several angles. One of the simplest methods of classification is by means of the elements. That is to say *Keser* is considered to be Air, *Chokmah* is Fire, and *Binah* is Water. These three constitute the first and most important triad. It is considered that this triad reflects itself downwards so that the elements make a sort of criss-cross pattern. Thus we have *Chesed* reflect-ing the Water from *Binah*, *Gevurah* reflecting the Fire from

Chokmah and *Tipharas* reflecting the Air down the Middle Pillar from *Keser*. This completes the second triad, which again reflects itself downwards as in a mirror. *Netzach* reflects the Fire from *Gevurah*, *Hod*, the Water from *Chesed*, and *Yesod*, the Air from

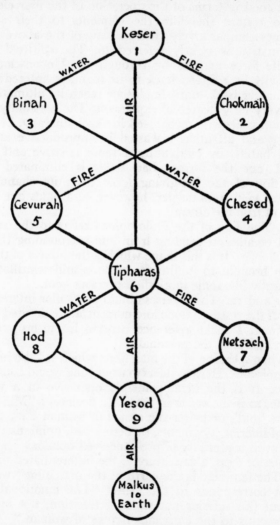

Fig. 2.—THE ELEMENTS ON THE TREE

Tipharas. Here we have the third triad, which reflects itself and forms a new element, the combination and base of all the others, Earth in *Malkus.* Thus, as the simplest means of classification, the entire universe and man himself may be understood in terms of the operation of the four elements.

To restore therefore the elements to their superiors becomes comparatively clear in view of the above scheme. Sublimation is clearly referred to. The spiritual energy, the life force manifesting through the Unconscious, must gradually be referred back to its manifest antecedent, and this further back, until finally we reach its ultimate source or a very lofty degree of expression. The possibility of sublimation is likewise recognized in Psychotherapy. For where energy and attention is wasted in unproductive and anti-social habits, by cultivating a more creative and socially useful one the former bad habit is eliminated by the deviation of the life-giving force from its channel. The magical view goes deeper, however, and holds out a better hope of true usefulness.

8. The Egg of the Philosophers refers to the aura, the ovoid emanation exuding from and surrounding the astro-mental form. It is this shape which is the subject of the work. When brought to fulfilment, it glows and scintillates most brilliantly like some more than precious gem.

11 and 12. These verses obtain particular interest in the light of the research done and nomenclature decided upon by Dr. Jung. I make reference here to his terms *anima* and *animus*, parts of the personality.

When speaking of the masculine which is "the heaven of the feminine", Hermes refers to what Jung would consider the *animus*. It is the ideal principle operative in a woman's psyche, as is the *anima* in man. He declares : "Mind makes up the 'soul', or better the *animus* of woman . . . (it) consists of inferior judgments, or better said, opinions . . . (it) consists in a plurality of pre-conceived opinions . . . (it) is an inferior *logos*, a caricature of the differentiated mind."

"The feminine is the earth of the masculine" without a doubt corresponds to the *anima*. "The emotional nature of man (his inferior not superior function, not his mind) corresponds to the conscious nature of woman." That is, therefore, the ground whereon his conscious psyche may function. *Anima* Jung further defines "as an image, or archetype or as the resultant of all the experiences of man with woman. . . ." It represents the emotional and feeling aspect of his psyche. "I have defined the *anima* in a man," continues he, "as a personification of the unconscious in general, and have therefore taken it as a bridge to the unconscious, that is, the function of relationship to the unconscious." See also the two large coloured diagrams in Vol. I of *The Golden Dawn*, which extend these concepts.

13. A vast amount of material exists in early psychoanalytical literature on the subject and significance of the Dragon. A great deal of this is well synthesized in *The Psychology of the Unconscious* by Jung. Briefly it may be said that the Dragon refers to the instincts, to undomesticated libido. We have already defined the libido not as sexual desire alone as the Freudians claim, but as the sum total of all psychic energy, the life force peculiar to any organism. Undomesticated libido would therefore represent that portion of psychic energy which has not yet been recognized and hence employed by consciousness. In consequence, it remains in a crude, undeveloped, unutilized and undomesticated state. Adding to this condition the psychic state of fear and anxiety which so to speak poisons this energy, it comes to represent a source of real danger to the individual. Whatever within cannot be dealt with invariably becomes a psychic projection, an objective something which the undeveloped psyche can suppress, or from which it may make frantic efforts to escape, or deal with in other ways.

All primitive and archaic concepts of the devil, satan, evil, etc., represent just such projected or objectified psychic energy that has not been recognized nor included within the scope of the ego. Ignorance as to its true nature gives rise to further fear, and this emotion invests the psychic object with innumerable qualities and predicates born and bred from fantasy. The dragon, which is precisely such a projection of feared because untamed psychic energy and content, is symbolic of the instinctual nature. It represents enormous power and dynamic energy, the emotional drives and urges which are at the foundation and root of all conscious development. Accepted and thus brought within the possibility of development and utilization—for denial and

E

repression transforms it into a fearful life-rending monster—
it serves as a trained and faithful beast whereupon the
psyche may ride and proceed upon its individual evolution.

One alchemical commentator defines the dragon as "the
self-willed spirit, which is externally derived into nature, by
the fall into generation". That is to say, summarily, the
instinctual life divorced from the higher and intellectual
faculties.

In another text *Coelum Terrae* by Thomas Vaughan, given
in Book Three of this work, there is the following with
reference to the nature of the Dragon :

> I am a poisonous dragon, present everywhere and
> to be had for nothing. My water and fire dissolve and
> compound. Out of my body thou shalt draw the Green
> and the Red Lion ; but if thou dost not exactly know
> me thou wilt—with my fire—destroy thy five senses. A
> most pernicious, quick poison comes out of my nostrils
> which hath been the destruction of many. Separate
> therefore the thick from the thin artificially, unless
> thou dost delight in extreme poverty. I give thee faculties
> both male and female and the powers both of heaven
> and earth. The mysteries of my art are to be performed
> magnanimously and with great courage, if thou wouldst
> have me overcome the violence of the fire, in which
> attempt many have lost both their labour and their
> substance. I am the egg of Nature known only to the
> wise, such as are pious and modest, who make of me a
> little world. Ordained I was by the Almighty God for
> men, but—though many desire me—I am given only to
> few, that they may relieve the poor with my treasures
> and not set their minds in gold that perisheth. I am
> called of the philosophers Mercury ; my husband is
> gold philosophical. I am the old dragon that is present
> everywhere on the face of the earth. I am father and
> mother, youthful and ancient, weak and yet most
> strong, life and death, visible and invisible, hard and
> soft, descending to the earth, and ascending to the
> heavens, most high and most low, light and heavy.
> In me the order of Nature is oftentimes inverted—in
> colour, number, weight and measure. I have in me the

light of Nature ; I am dark and bright ; I spring from the earth and I come out of heaven ; I am well known and yet a mere nothing ; all colours shine in me and all metals by the beams of the sun. I am the Carbuncle of the Sun, a most noble clarified earth, by which thou mayst turn copper, iron, tin, and lead into most pure gold.

Our present text states that all the principles of man are polluted by the dragon—by an anxiety and fear-laden Unconscious. The instinctual expression at the base of the individual life when ill-understood is distinctly poisonous and dangerous. It is evident that every attempt to classify such a condition must be in terms of evil and blackness. Hence a blackness pollutes the very nature of man so long as he remains subject to the unconscious psyche, and dominated by its impulses—which latter in any event, by reason of repression and confused thinking and feeling, are false and untrue. Even the mind, rational and logical as it may seem, is not exempt from this pollution. Its very habits and its "exact" methods of thinking, its intellectual predilections, are coloured and compulsively motivated by the emotional repressions. As Hermes remarks, "By it (the blackness) he (the dragon) ascends into the air"— air being the element representing the intellectual and rational life. So long as this unrighteous condition prevails, by just so long is man deluded as to the real nature of the universe and of his own interior possibilities. It prevents him from ever becoming aware of his destiny, and of integrating himself. This perpetual tendency to schizophrenia is precisely that which renders him mortal and incapable of living consciously and divinely for his own high spiritual ends beyond physical death.

Hence our text advises us what to do. A dissolution of the entire emotional and mental nature is to be achieved before we can proceed. The hovering vapour is to be removed from the Water, from the Philosopher's Mercury, which is the inner intelligence, before the latter can perceive life clearly and accurately. The blackness requires elimination from the oily tincture—the emotions must be cleansed and purified following a full-blooded acceptance of their existence. Then they may shine forth in daily life for what they truly are, the fire of life. Death dies from the faeces, the substantial vehicle of the above, by the same sort of achievement. As soon as the emotional and feeling principle functions cleanly in its own right, and the mind's perceptions and functions are enhanced by a divorce from automatic emotional and instinctual compulsion, then also their sheath undergoes a transformation. We know what tremendous changes can be wrought upon the physical body through neurosis and repression. We are also aware how functional and organic diseases and neurotic symptoms fall away under psychotherapeutic treatment. How much more so should not the ethereal vestment of the inner man react to a more perfectly functioning psyche? Such is the reward promised by the Golden Treatise.

14. Oils and sulphurs are here identified. Both become synonymous of the emotional life, and the libido which fires it. One commentator here remarks, "The knowledge of this secret sulphur, and how to prepare it and use it in this work includes the whole art of perfection. It is the stirrer-up of the whole power and efficacy and purifier of the matter ; hence Hermes calls it the Perscrutinator, eminently distinguishing the Rational Ferment". Here our commentator prefers to look upon Sulphur as a mental rather than an emotional principle.

17. The Stone—the integrated and perfected mind functioning easily and unimpeded in a newly constructed etheric vehicle—is quite evidently composed of various elements, etc. But in order to produce the Philosopher's Stone, the elements as found in their natural state in the natural unillumined man, must be divided, dissevered, and broken down. For the elements in this world, so far from being simple, are compounded. There is no water that is only water ; no fire that is only fire, nor any known earthly element that is complete or single by itself ; no gas is complete in itself. The elements, therefore, in this world are all now compounded, mortal, subject to division—adulterated and mixed. After dividing and dissevering them, it will be possible to reassemble those principles and elements on an entirely new pattern for the further development of the individual.

18. The disintegration accomplished, it is the freed Mind united to its *anima*, forming a complete and re-integrated psyche, which is the key of the restoration. A new heaven and a new earth. No wonder Hermes apostro-phizes the virtue of this healing water ! The regenerate soul *does* have the power to heal and to save—a mind cleansed by analysis, aware of its own true essence, made strong by the union with its *anima*, and filled with the influx of the awakened vital spirit, the libido. Here are the keys of Wisdom.

CHAPTER FOUR

THOMAS VAUGHAN, in his *Lumen de Lumine*, describes the stage mentioned at the opening of the third section even more eloquently than Hermes: "Thou must incamp against them with the fire of nature, and be sure thou dost bring thy line round about. Circle them in, and stop all avenues, that they find no relief. Continue this siege patiently."

The "binding" that Hermes recommends must be a similar operation. It would refer to an advanced stage of self-immersion, when consciousness is withdrawn from all the avenues of sense and perception. A meditation or introversion which has become deep and profound could be described in very much these terms. And if we refer to oriental texts and philosophies of Yoga and concentration, we shall discover that it is in the deepest meditations that the spinal Spirit-Fire—which is called the Paraclete in the New Testament, Speirema by the Gnostics, and Kundalini by the Yogis—is aroused. It is in such a deep indrawn condition that the philosopher's matter contends with fire.

The psychological approach hereto would be that in profound states of introversion, when there is no leakage of the attention on the objective plane, the focus of the entire field of attention is directed within. The levels of consciousness within the psyche itself become the object of perception. As a result of this inseeing, the contents of these levels became invaded by the stream of libido up-welling from the deepest levels of the Unconscious.

Since the Unconscious has a vehicle of its own type of substance, then the "washed bodies" refer to the vehicle of the Unconscious, and the "spirits" to the vital energic current of libido.

4. In order once more to confuse the ignorant and unworthy, Hermes harks back to the beginning in this

inconsequential way. Unconscious of the existence of the Stone of the Philosopher's within—no better term than Unconscious could have been devised to express this condition of ignorance—how else that mankind should defile this great seminal treasure, the seed of immortality. Hence the allusion to the dunghill.

We strain the psychological method to the point of breaking in our attempt to understand the reference to two Argent-vives. We know that the process of analysis affects not only the patient or analysand but also the analyst. Groddeck has gone so far as to say that it is the analyst who benefits or learns most. Jung also writes that the analyst

> is as much a part of the psychic process of the treatment as is the patient, and is equally exposed to the trans-forming influences. Indeed, if the doctor is more or less inaccessible to this influence, he is correspondingly robbed of his influence over the patient; if he is influenced only consciously, he shows a defect of consciousness which prevents him from seeing the patient clearly. The fourth stage of analytical psychology, then, demands not only the transformation of the patient, but also the counter-application to himself by the doctor of the system which he prescribes in any given case.

There must be a mutual interplay and interaction between the Unconscious of both analyst and patient. For any lasting good to be done to the one, an effect must be produced in the other. Seen in this light, psychotherapy is a mutually conducted procedure of intense human value. No longer is it the cold distant scientific process envisaged some thirty years ago.

5. We now approach rebirth symbolism of a curious pictorial and eloquent character. That the union of male and female produces offspring in the biological world is a commonplace fact. But it has similar application in the psychological world. The union of an integrated psyche—the "crowned king"—with the principle of instinct and feeling—"our red daughter", formerly latent and dormant within, must be a pleasurable and highly emotional ex-perience. In literature written by mystics and religious

enthusiasts we have panegyrics and emotional tributes
to the bliss and ecstasy of the mystical experience or divine
union. Just as the abreaction of repressed material is
accompanied by an emotional storm, so the union of these
two psychic factors is likewise characterized by an intensity
of feeling, and by a release of enormous energy expressing
itself in terms of Light and Fire. A gentle fire, not hurtful,
is quite an appropriate expression for such an intensity
of feeling. The psyche conceives a spiritual child—a son,
conjoined with and yet superior to both its parents. It is not,
naturally, an objective product visible to the eyes of the
world. But it inheres within the psychic domain as an
integral part of the psyche, as a spontaneous effort to
transcend itself in a higher, more inclusive synthesis. Just
as the crowned king is the *Ruach* centred in *Tipharas*—the
Sun is its Father—so the red daughter is a symbolic glyph
of the instinctive world in the guise of a female form—its
Mother the Moon. So the child is *Daás*, knowledge, the
Ruach reborn as the supernal child of the Middle Pillar,
the direct result of the overcoming of the red dragon, the
child of Wisdom and Understanding. Once more I must
refer the reader to the large coloured plates in Vol. I of
The Golden Dawn.

The continuance of a life attitude in a balanced rational
manner, adhering throughout to the middle way, is calculated to produce an abiding peace, an inner contentment,
and harmony. It is a sense of intense happiness and satisfaction radiating from some deep interior source. It is a
realization of the harmony within accepting the harmony
without. It is this tranquillity of soul and spirit which is the
true characteristic of integrity, of wholeness, of saintlike
holiness. And it is this which stabilizes the newly formed
Quintessence, the recently born child within.

The "boundary of hearts" is the object sought for
and which satisfies when attained, remarks Mrs. Atwood.
In this sense it represents the descent of the Light of the
Supernals, an extraordinary heightening and clarification
of consciousness. This heightening of consciousness accompanied by a deep intensity of feeling perpetuates and
consolidates the attainment. As the text says, with reference
to the Son, "Then is he transformed, and his tincture by

help of the fire remains red as flesh." It matures and ripens as an individual point of view—attaining full fruition as an habitual and not an occasional high outlook. Not only is this so but a marked effect is wrought on the invisible vehicle of consciousness. In a former quotation from Thomas Vaughan's *Coelum Terrae* we found the following as a finale to an exalted panegyric : "All colours shine in me and all metals by the beams of the sun. I am the Carbuncle of the Sun." Hence the colour change manifesting in the aura must be predominately a deep-red one, so that it glows and emits a brilliant rubified light.

6. Clearly the attainment spells the eclipse of the Dragon. Where light shines no darkness can there abide. For being the basis of the instinctual life, harnessed and chained to the needs and clearly perceived ideals of the psyche, the dragon shuns the sunbeams and the daylight. No longer do its projections and compulsive automatisms haunt the light of consciousness. No longer is the personality tortured as by some foul and evil presence. Its needs and dictates, once so imperious, cease their urgency, finding their proper place within the natural economy.

The "occult treasures" are, as the text itself makes clear, no more nor less than the manifestation of the Son. He is the Stone of the Philosophers—not yet, even now, however, brought to final perfection. But at any rate the stage reached is so exalted as possibly to bring about the frequently encountered feeling that finality is reached. Using Christian symbolism, this would indicate that Christ has been born within the heart, manifesting the glory of his godhead within the entire personality.

Hermes further remarks that "the virgin's milk is whitened". The alchemical Salt, the astral substance of the interior design body, about to be glorified and made radiant, has not yet attained full maturity. The reference to virgin's milk again demands a quotation which is highly expressive and illuminative from Vaughan's *Coelum Terrae* with regard to the First Matter :

> It is a most pure sweet virgin, for nothing as yet hath been generated out of her. But if at any time she breeds it is by the fire of Nature for that is her

husband. She is no animal, or vegetable, no mineral, neither is she extracted out of animals, vegetables, or minerals, but she is pre-existent to them all, for she is the mother of them. Yet one thing I must say : she is not much short of life, for she is almost animal. Her composition is miraculous and different from all other compounds whatsoever. Gold is not so compact but every sophister concludes it is no simple ; but she is so much that no one man believes she is more. She yields to nothing but love, for her end is generation and that was never yet performed by violence. He that knows how to wanton and toy with her, the same shall receive all her treasures. First, she sheds at her nipples a thick heavy water, but white as any snow ; the philosophers call it Virgin's Milk. Secondly, she gives him blood from her very heart ; it is a quick, heavenly fire ; some improperly call it their sulphur. Thirdly and lastly, she presents him with a secret crystal, of more worth and lustre than the white rock and all her rosials. This is she, and these are her favours ; catch her, if you can.

7. But the next verse carries us a step further. By itself, and with the passage of time, the Son grows and becomes reddened and full grown and mature. "The Son is invested with the red garment and the purple is put on."

This final stage is worthy of comparison with a description written by the great Gnostic poet Bardesanes. He describes in a poem the descent of the soul into the realms of matter, and its ultimate reascent. G. R. S. Mead translated it as *Vol. X* of his *Echoes from Gnosis Series*, and it is called *The Hymn of the Robe of Glory*. It is too long to quote in its entirety, but I give certain lines from the end :

I saw it (a bright robe sent by his parents) making
    itself ready.
I heard the sound of its tones,
And I perceived also in myself
That my stature was growing according to his labours.
It was spreading itself out towards me,
It hastened that I might take it on.
And I stretched forth and received it,
With the beauty of its colours I adorned myself.

And my toga of brilliant colours
I cast around me, in its whole breadth.
I clothed myself therewith, and ascended
To the Majesty of my Father who had sent it to me.
And I was with him in his kingdom.
And he promised me also that to the gate
Of the King of Kings I should speed with him,
And bringing my gift and my pearl
I should appear with him before our King.

The opening versicle of the fourth section can best
be understood, I think, by quoting Mrs. Atwood's footnote :

The fermenting light, by constant addition of the
spirit, leavens more and more, increasing as it tends to
the perception of the final cause in life. As Solomon,
speaking of the Divine Wisdom, says, "Exalt her and she
shall promote thee. She shall bring thee to honour when
thou dost embrace her." (Prov. iv, 8–9.)

At the stage when the psychic integration has been
achieved, it is needful that man should be so simple in
his childlike and complete acceptance of life that he is
attentive and obedient to the higher dictates of his
heightened consciousness. To disregard such dictates would
in the long run be tantamount wilfully to destroying the
communion established between the different levels of the
psyche, and would imply a return to the former neurotic
condition. But by obedience, as it were, to himself, an
unconditional acceptance of himself, he helps the Stone,
his psyche. The result is that it helps him and protects him
so that all his works prosper and flourish. It is considerably
reminiscent in certain senses of that mystical treatise
The Light on the Path, where we read :

Stand aside in the coming battle, and though thou
fightest be not thou the warrior. Look for the Warrior
and let him fight in thee. . . . He is thyself, yet infinitely wiser and stronger than thyself. Look for him, else
in the fever and hurry of the fight thou mayest pass him,
and he will not know thee unless thou knowest him.

But to know him and to protect him first, as in the case of the Stone, is the essential that later he too may help and protect.

5. Venus is a goddess of the same kind as Hera, Isis, Rhea, etc. All are *anima* figures—love goddesses, and from the Qabalistic point of view are referred to the Sephirah *Binah*, the Great Sea and the Mother. Venus and Aphrodite in Greek mythology are depicted as having sprung from the sea. There is another series of correspondence which identifies Venus with the occult cohesive influence joining *Chokmah* to *Binah*, the interior Father imago to the Mother, Wisdom to Understanding. As such she must represent the love of the one for the other. And she represents as the higher love which is understanding, the means of entry into the interior Supernal life. We have here an adumbration of a religious or mystical technique of devotion. *Bhakta* or love is, according to many schools of mysticism, the supreme and ineffable means of divine union—that is to say of integration. Since *Binah* also is *Shekinah*, the Holy Spirit; the manifestation of which is always described in the symbolism of fire and light, such symbolism also pertains therefore to Venus, as the text itself advises. Love and fire and the means of integration have thus a necessary and categorical connection.

In Egyptian symbolism, Osiris was not only the husband but the brother of the heavenly Isis. From their marriage the divine child Horus was born. The text repeats the desirability of such an incestuous relationship, referring to the newly arisen as Venus' brother and that nothing could be better or more venerable than that they should be conjoined.

From the practical point of view, the analysand, after having achieved a certain degree of integration through a union with his own instinctive and emotional processes, may well consider analysis and the process of development at an end. His too urgent emotional demands have become quiescent because understood, and his neurotic symptoms have subsided. But a higher principle still remains concealed and latent within. Mrs. Atwood's footnote to this verse is : "And when she (Venus) appears, the artist is rejoiced, and thinks perhaps his work is finished, and that he has the treasure of the world in hand; but it is not so; for if he tries it the light still will be found imperfect, alone, and transient, without the masculine tincture to fix it in manifestation."

6. The attainment becomes fixed, as a permanent possibility by a further union. Just as the first stage comprised a unification of consciousness with its instinctual basis to form a united whole, so now the psyche must open itself to the Light and wisdom and understanding of the Supernals or to the primordial archetypes of the Collective Unconscious. Such a union completes its nature, rendering it capable of enduring and persisting, since it has achieved a conscious union with its own eternal and immortal essence.

In occult symbolism, a male force is spoken of as a sudden, sharp, and abrupt force, powerful yet without the ability to persist. A feminine force on the contrary is slow, stable, receptive, and enduring. The one is the throne or seat of activity of the other, and the best results, so far as lasting effects are concerned, are obtained by uniting the two types of force. Hermes implies a similar union. For though the freed psyche, the king, is crowned and adorned with the diadem, it is only by being chained to the arms and breast of his mother—to Venus, his sister and wife, the higher soul—that his substance keeps together. The love of Venus acts as a cohesive force, for otherwise the power of the king's attainment would soon be dissipated, and the virtue would soon depart from consciousness, which would thus exist without a firm foundation.

8. The simplest elemental attribution, discussed on a former page, helps a little here. *Binah* is the Great Sea, the element of Water, and is therefore blue, but because of its Saturnine attribution is also indigo or black. *Chokmah* is Wisdom, and the element of Fire, red in colour. Whilst *Keser* is the spirit of Life, the source of all things, circulating in all things, and is referred to the element of Air, and its colour is yellow.

The verse recalls Mrs. Atwood's definition of the Hermetic Art. "Alchemy *is* philosophy ; it is *the* philosophy, the seeking out of The Sophia in the mind."

Hermes says, "Behold I have obscured the matter treated of, by circumlocution, depriving it of light. I have termed this dissolved and this joined, this nearest I have termed furthest off." The Hermetic authors indulged freely in circumlocution and every artifice of cunning in order to deceive the unwary and those they considered unworthy of their art. It is this that has made the study of alchemy so difficult.

Elsewhere, the crow has been defined as the Bird of Hermes. It signifies thereby the animal soul, brain, or body consciousness itself. On the other hand, we would do well to consider every correspondence or association that the word calls up. As a black bird, the colour is significant. Black is the colour of death, of evil, of impurity. Uniting the two concepts, it is evident that from several points of view consciousness is considered black or evil in its natural state, because it is precisely that which blinds our eyes to God as the alchemists would put it, or which prevents us from perceiving the true nature of life. "The mind is the slayer of reality", another mystical book observes, counselling the disciple therefore "to slay the slayer". This evokes that difference between Occidental and Oriental views of religious aspiration which I had occasion to note above. It is a characteristic of the West to make goodness issue from that which is evil. If the mind blinds us to the true nature of reality, and is evil, does it behove us to destroy the mind itself? This idea was never compatible to the practical outlook of the Western religious philosophers. They argued to the contrary. We know that the ego has certain uses and functions. In its own sphere it is a useful instrument built up through long aeons of evolution for our benefit. Let us then proceed from where Nature left off and perfect by our own achievement the instrument with which she has endowed us. If our present ego is evil, let us cleanse and refine this ego, eliminating the evil, the dross, and confusion so that, where it failed in its prior state, it may serve us faithfully and well when placed in its proper sphere. Similar is the attitude of Hermes. Though the crow, the black bird of sorrow and foreboding and ill-omen, the mind in all its complacency and confused chaotic thinking, is evil, nevertheless what it yields following its deliberate decapitation is the beginning of this art. The child of so awful a parent must possess enormous possibilities.

Another point of view, more mystical in nature, also presents itself in interpretation of the phrase "what is born of the crow is the beginning of this art". Referring to a work by Porphyry, Mrs. Atwood justly observes in her *Suggestive Inquiry into the Hermetic Mystery* that :

> There is a twofold death ; the one indeed universally known, in which the body is liberated from the soul ; but the other peculiar to philosophers in which the soul is liberated from the body ; nor does the one entirely follow the other. That which nature binds, nature also dissolves ; that which the soul binds, the soul likewise can dissolve ; nature, indeed, binds the body to the soul, but the soul binds herself to the body. Nature therefore liberates the body from the soul, but the soul may also liberate herself from the body. That is to say, if she know how, and have the right disposition awarded, she may dissolve her own conceptive vehicle, even the parental bond, and return consciously (the elementary principles remaining, nor yet suffered to depart) under the dominion of another law to life. That was the way to "precious death", spoken of by the Hebrews and Academics, this the "happy gate of blackness" celebrated by the old adepts, the "head of Hermes' crow", which is in the beginning of the work.

The emphasis here is placed on the art of meditation which, carried to the point when consciousness is completely withdrawn into itself, induces a trance state in which all bodily form and limitation is surmounted so that it ascends to an intimate contact with divinity. Plotinus of the Neo-platonic school, and the methods of the Hindu Yogis, illustrate this point of view perfectly. Meditation was the means employed to penetrate the barrier of consciousness, thus permitting the vital stream of life and living experience to well up spontaneously from the unconscious levels of the mind.

2. The horse is a universal symbol of the Mother. This again is an objective symbol for the Unconscious, the animal life, since it is from thence that consciousness is born. Again, the horse in astrological symbolism corresponds

to the zodiacal sign Sagittarius which represents aspiration and spiritual yearning. Associated with this idea there is the *Chaldean Oracle* :

> Also there is the Vision of the fire-flashing courser of Light, or also a child borne aloft on the shoulders of the celestial steed, fiery, or clothed with Gold, or naked, or shooting with the bow shafts of Light, and standing on the shoulders of the Horse. But if thy meditation prolongeth itself thou shalt unite all these Symbols in the form of a Lion.

Nearly all animals, from the psychological viewpoint, indicate libido or instinct, the type and size of animal indicating the degree of its domesticity. Speed in running is the chief characteristic of the horse. Its tendency when frightened to bolt with the bit between its teeth is another. These are fairly descriptive symbols of the primitive instinctive principle inhering within each one of us.

The alchemical writers inform us that those who search for urine and faeces are assuredly on the wrong track. That which comes forth from the horse's belly is certainly urine and dung. But what is the characteristic of these ? What is the symbolical meaning denoted and played upon by these writers ? Clearly, they refer to a moist heat. It is this which renders explicable the phrase that Hermes employs.

The dissolved elements are transformed by a slow gentle heating into what is called the "Dragon eating his own wings and destroying himself". At this juncture, it is worth quoting a similar process from Vaughan :

> Continue this siege patiently, and they turn into an ugly venomous black toad ; which will be transformed to a horrible devouring dragon creeping and weltering in the bottom of her cave, without wings. Touch her not by any means, not so much as with thy hands, for there is not upon earth such a vehement transcendent poison.

We have already defined the dragon as the libido, undomesticated, weighted down by the burden of anxiety, guilt, and fear, effects which are repressed into the Unconscious. The effect of this siege, of introversion or meditation, is to turn anxiety against anxiety. The dissolved constituents of the broken-down astro-mental form vie and war one with another. During psychotherapeutic, or any medical treatment, for that matter, neurotic and psychotic symptoms apparently become much more severe. Anxiety increases to an alarming degree. In homeopathic treatment, any ailment is treated by such drugs and medicines as by themselves will duplicate the symptoms thrown up by the bodily system. Very often a physical or psychic crisis precipitates itself—much to the consternation, at first, of the patient. This psychic condition arrived at, the contents of consciousness, foul and sordid as they are—the scum on the glue-pot described by Geraldine Coster—evocative of shame, guilt, and anxiety when seen in their starkness, must be subjected to yet further analysis. The infantile reactions so out of place in an adult must be discarded and destroyed. A species of meditation must be engaged upon. All the senses must be closed to outgoing stimuli. The consciousness and its attention are to be completely withdrawn and focused inwards upon the hitherto hidden contents of its own nature. This is the furnace, the fire being the concentrated attention brought to bear on consciousness by meditation and introversion.

"Observe that none of the spirit may escape" may well imply that the critical attention is not to be permitted to wander from the unpleasant poisonous items included in consciousness. The libido must not leak out from this enclosed sphere of attention. It is all far too valuable. In any event, it comprises an integral part of the personality. And if any part, no matter how minute and apparently insignificant, of the spirit escapes that loss is irreparable and fatal to the concept of integrity and wholeness.

Silberer in his *Problems of Mysticism* has a word or two which is useful here :

> Patient effort is required. Precipitancy is as great an evil as inactivity. It is just as bad to scorch the tender blossoms by a forced and hasty fire (that in spite of its intensity may be merely a straw fire) as to let go out

F

the fire which should be continually kept alight, and to let grow cold the Mercury. The process of distillation is to be accomplished slowly, so that the spirit may not escape.

There is another viewpoint of alchemy, an ethical one, which is worthy of consideration. It finds its expression in :

> In the alembic of thy heart,
> Through the athanor of affliction,
> Seek thou the true stone of the wise.

Life and everyday experience are, by this interpretation, the means of initiation. It is the impact of life upon the soul, and the transmutation of sorrow within which develops an even attitude as an habitual reaction of the psyche. The heart here is the furnace, whilst affliction, that is to say the experience generally of this world, is the initiating fire.

3. As meditation and the introversion process deepen and become more profound, the heating of the psychic contents gives rise to a phenomenon which can only be described in terms similar to any physical one. "Hot air rises." That is to say, concentration, like a fiery ray turned inwards, heats the interior principles. The dormant libido, formerly con-. fined to the depths of the sea, rises to the higher levels, to the surface of consciousness.

What would be the effect of this libido ascent upon consciousness? Our text tells us. The brain, clearly, is the conscious intellectual life of the spirit. Sharp vinegar must without doubt refer to the libido, the vital living spirit. This assumption is justified in my mind by a significant allusion in a highly mystical and devotional treatise. Here, the spirit is represented as speaking metaphorically to the ego, its *persona*, in these words : "Wolf's bane is not so sharp as steel ; yet it pierceth the body more subtly. Even as evil kisses corrupt the blood, so do my words devour the spirit of man. I breathe, and there is infinite disease of the spirit. As an acid eats into steel, as a cancer that utterly corrupts the body ; so am I unto the spirit of man. I shall not rest until I have dissolved it all."

In a word, consciousness is dissolved and eaten up

by its impact with the upwelling libido from the unconscious psyche. Jung too observes that the impact of the narrow delimited yet intensely clear consciousness with the wide expanse of the Unconscious is disintegrative. Complexes and neurotic symptoms become changed considerably in their nature, which is to admit that the personality undergoes a marked transformation. The process, naturally, should be repeated again and again. Finally the point must be reached where in consciousness there is left no remnant at all of the elements causing suffering and conflict which formerly were so devastating and disturbing to the individual. Then only can a new life begin. Not until this freedom and liberation has been won can life be faced as it is, nor the nature of the world be seen in its true and intrinsic selfhood.

At the commencement of another cycle of recapitulation, Hermes reiterates the religious nature of the art, urging a spiritual point of view. How then could men have so deliberately misunderstood the terms of the art as to have fallen into the "torturing of metals" ? The mistaken steps of the "Puffers", as the false alchemists are known, who worried themselves to death with metals, minerals, and the most outrageous and unspeakable experiments, are here exposed by the author.

3. He states deliberately that the magical Form, wherein is concealed the unguent or elixir of Life, is within man himself in exactly the same sense as combustion is latent in combustible natures. It only awaits evocation.

4. The recapitulation proper is begun. Hermes signifies the two invisible poles of the quintessence wherein are implicit the three alchemical principles. The middle nature is the divine Mercury which reconciles the two opposites, and is the mediator between the heavenly fire of Sulphur and the earthy formative nature of Salt.

But, as the insistent author notes and has reminded us before, these principles and elements as they exist in their natural condition require purification. Nothing in nature is single and unadulterated. Gold when found is valueless until the grime and grit have been washed off, and the gold itself refined.

In magical working the same process stands out with

crystalline clearness. If the element Air is required for invocation purposes in Temple, then as a preliminary every element and every other force even including that particular element the Magus desires later to work with, has to be powerfully banished from the Circle. But the banishing over, and a pure and clear area obtained within the confines of the circle or Temple, then the element Air, for example, may be invoked with safety. For with a sure knowledge the Magus has made thoroughly certain that no other elements are present to adulterate it or render it mixed and impure.

5. Hence, from the natural principles inherent within the human constitution, Hermes demands the removal of all imperfections. The vapour from the water refers to the libido-residues developed from unrestrained infantile fantasy—impure thought-forms would be the appropriate occult cliché. And when this is accomplished, and the emotions and their vehicle are purified, then indeed we have "the sovereign philosophy and secret of all hidden things".

That some investigators have confounded the high art with metallurgical operations seems not very difficult to understand. The first verse of the seventh section would assuredly give some degree of authority and confirmation to their efforts. Yet the key is there. The terms need but simple translation. The seven bodies or metals are referrable to the seven astrological planets and these again to the constituents of man's own nature.

Saturn—lead—libido; synthetic symbol of (crude) unformulated spiritual nature.

Jupiter—tin—consciousness; memory in particular.

Mars—iron—will.

Venus—copper—Emotion, passion, and feeling.

Mercury—quicksilver—nervous force, prana, vital magnetism.

Luna—silver—the astral; the quick ever-changing substance which is the vehicle of consciousness, plastic to every passing thought.

Sol—gold—Soul; the redeemed and regenerated ego.

When purified by art, and illuminated by the processes of Alchemy, indeed consciousness may transmute all the other metals, or principles, in man. Transforming them, it enables them to perform their perfect and proper function in the psychic economy without hindrance, and without interference from any other—uniting them all into a single whole.

2. The ferment, here described, is none other than the vital spirit, libido. It alone, when assisted in its ascent from the darkling depths of the underworld, can so affect the different parts of the psyche as to act after the nature of a ferment—and to transform them. Unity of the individuality is indispensable to the commencement of the transforming action—otherwise we have not fermentation, but disintegration and chaos.

5. The result of integration may at first be bewildering in so far as life then presents itself in a totally different guise to the unsuspecting sight of the experimentalist. He has finished with the old neurotic point of view, but has entered a world where he is not yet certain of himself. It is a temporary state of doubt and perplexity. That is, it is not sweet. But it is only a temporary stopping place, soon yielding when familiarity accustoms vision to that which is strange, to a more settled and therefore happier and more balanced outlook.

BOOK TWO

BOOK TWO

CHAPTER FIVE

THE MAGNETIC THEORY

THERE is but little question that the application of the psychological method, though it does explain much, does not fully cover the ground in alchemy in a way that is particularly satisfying to the critical sense. Possibly, we should be content in that it affords us some degree of empirical understanding and insight into obscure modes of thought. We are given a certain degree of perception into what are otherwise objectionable forms of obscurantism and secrecy. It seems offensive to our particular modern type of consciousness that men, otherwise of good character, sound intellectual judgment and capacity, should in the past have expressed no small degree of sympathy with this subject. Their sympathy and enthusiasm receives therefore some approbation and justification when interpreting their mystifications in this particular light.

Analytical Psychology and its fellow, Psycho-analysis, are quite recent appearances on the threshold of intellectual accomplishment. In mediaeval times we find but little evidence of the psychological method. Of philosophies there have been dozens. Former epochs abounded with mystical systems of interior prayer and meditation, and Magic too was well represented. It is in the past, in my estimation, and in ancient systems, that we must look for another and possibly more enlightening clue to the hermetic mystery. In fact, one author, Mrs. M. Atwood, who has given us what indubitably must be admitted to be the best volume on alchemical hermeneutics, does posit the theory that Mesmerism or Magnetism gives the key—though no more —to this mystery. In view of this hypothesis, therefore, it may be wise if I summarily consider the historical ground and antecedents of vital Magnetism in order that the reader may be acquainted with the outlines of what later will be elaborated.

From a study of Greek and Latin literature it is almost certain that a species of healing by a laying on of hands was so commonly practised in ancient days as not to demand a detailed or particularized description. Underlying such a method was the belief that the human organism generates or is permeated by an electric or creative power or fluid, animal magnetism or vital emanation. Not only does it circulate in its own arterial system but, aided by a laying on of hands and directed by a keen imagination and strong will, it can be communicated to another person for therapeutic purposes. It need hardly be laboured that the Bible contains many references to cures of an apparently magnetic nature. And such magnetic methods continued from the earliest times through to the Middle Ages. They were commonplace in Europe for centuries.

Avicenna, a physician of the ninth or tenth century, said : "The imagination of man can act not only on his own body, but even on others and very distant bodies. It can fascinate and modify them ; make them ill, or restore them to health." Marcus Fienus, a physician of Florence, said in the same century : "A vapour, or a certain spirit, emitted by the rays of the eyes, or in any other manner, can take effect on a person near you. It is not to be wondered at that diseases of the mind and of the body should be communicated or cured in that manner."

Petrus Pomponatius of Mantua believed that : "Some men are specially endowed with eminently curative faculties ; the effects produced by their touch are wonderful ; but even touch is not always necessary ; their glances, their mere intention of doing good, are efficient to the restoration of health." Here we have an adumbration, at least, of hypnotic practise and the suggestion theory.

Van Helmont, the sixteenth-century discoverer of laudanum, ammonia, volatile salts, etc., also held opinions similar to Mesmer. He held that : "Magnetism is a universal agent ; there is nothing new in it but the name. Magnetism is that occult influence which bodies exert over each other at a distance by means of attraction and repulsion." He named this influence the "Magnale Magnum", as Eliphas Levi much later on, in the nineteenth century, spoke of it as the Astral Light. Helmont conceived of it, not as a corporeal thing, but as an ethereal, pure, vital spirit or essence. It penetrates all bodies, and in man has its seat in the blood, where it exists as a peculiar energy, enabling him by the force of will and imagination to act at a distance. He also asserted the idea of polarity or the duality of magnetism, which he claims is composed of a vital principle and a "will principle". The former exists "in the flesh and blood of man", the latter belongs to the soul, or consciousness. But since soul and body are not separate discrete entities but together comprise a whole, so magnetism is one, manifesting in different principles on different planes. It seems to accord fairly well with the psychological definitions of libido.

Sendivogius, the great alchemist, wrote : "Let therefore the searcher of this sacred science know that the soul in man, the lesser world or microcosm, substituting the place of its centre, is the king, and is placed in the vital spirit in the purest blood. That governs the mind, and the mind the body." It is upon this statement, and the philosophy underlying such a postulate, that is built up the hypothesis of vital magnetism as the key opening to the threshold of the alchemical mystery.

William Maxwell, a contemporary of Van Helmont, held similar views, some of which are curiously like those of emanations or radiations from the body, countenanced openly in several modern scientific quarters. He remarks : "All bodies emit corporeal rays serving as vehicles through which the soul transmits her influence, by communicating to them her energy and power of acting ; and these rays are not only corporeal, but they are even composed of various kinds of matter. The universal remedy is no other than the vital spirit strengthened in a suitable subject."

Sebastian Wirdig, a learned philosopher-physician of the same generation, averred : "The whole world exists through magnetism ; all sublunary vicissitudes occur through magnetism ; life is preserved by magnetism ; everything functions by magnetism."

Similar passages are to be found in the works of Paracelsus and a host of leading authors of these and later centuries. All more or less affirm the existence of a universal ether, the medium both of light and thought activity.

That ether they represented interiorly in man by a vital spirit or magnetism which radiated and emanated a vital influence from him, subtly and invisibly. This spiritual force, so the theory went, could be controlled and manipulated for purposes of healing by a willed transmission through the hands, or by direct glance of the eye, to another ailing individual. But it is only when we come to Mesmer and his disciples and colleagues that we realize the superiority of his theoretical formulation of the concept of magnetism and the advantages of his particular approach.

Franz Anton Mesmer was born in Austria in 1734, and in 1766 in Vienna he became an M.D. His inaugural address maintained that the sun, moon, and stars affect each other and cause tides, not only in the ocean and sea, but in the atmosphere too. It was his theory that they affect in a similar way all organized bodies, through the medium of a subtle and mobile fluid which he conceived to pervade and permeate the universe, and to associate all things together in material intercourse and harmony. His theory further included the idea that all things soever in Nature possess a peculiar power which manifests itself by special action upon other bodies. That is to say, it is a physical and dynamic power acting exteriorly, without any chemical union, or without being introduced physically into the interior of the organization. Mesmer also contemplated the idea that all organic bodies, animals, plants, trees, waters, metals, might be magnetized. By this he meant that they could be charged or impregnated with a flow or current of vital energy. This cosmic vitality or animal magnetism could be transmitted, he claimed, by direct contact with a body already magnetized, or by means of the hand, the look, or even the will. Like light and electricity it could penetrate solid and fluid bodies, and, so he thought, could be reflected by mirrors, or polished surfaces, especially in the direction of its poles.

So far as the practical application of general theory is concerned, Mesmer, like modern psychological exponents, believed that moral causes and erroneous attitudes towards life may constitute the underlying factors in disease. That is to say an attitude towards life which was in conflict or at variance with reality could interfere with the psychic distribution of vitality throughout the bodily system. Such a general equilibrium could produce vastly improved health in functional and organic disease. His theory held that the magnetism is continually circulating in the bodily system. Not only so but that it emanates to an appreciable distance about the body. When the rapport is made between patient and healer, that is when contact is established either by glance or mesmeric passes or physical touch, it circulates through the systems of the two people, just as blood would if their arteries and veins were interconnected—assuming that such a condition were possible.

The reception of his theories and then startling cures was not particularly happy. Commissions were authorized to examine the cures announced by Mesmer and his patients, and following unfavourable reports and much antagonism he fell foul of public opinion almost everywhere. In passing, it may be well to mention that somehow or other in the early part of his career he had received some suggestive ideas from two Jesuits named Gassner and Hehl. The former used exorcism as a means of curing certain types of disease. He held a theory, modified from the straightforward Roman Catholic view, that there are two kinds of disease. The one is curable by the ordinary means employed by doctors, whilst the other can only be cured by priestly means, by exorcism. To these he added a third category which he called "mixed", requiring the services both of priest and doctor. Gassner also imparted the secret of strengthening the curative effect by moving one's hands over the diseased parts of the body. Later such movements became known as "passes". From Hehl, Mesmer had obtained at the outset of his public career a set of magnetized steel plates which, when laid upon different parts of the body, were claimed to have a curative effect. Mesmer did not long persist in the use of these plates, passing on to the use of his baquet, and much later on discarding all these accessories, coming to rely exclusively on the magnetism generated by or emanating from his own personality. He pictured man as a closed circuit of the magnetic fluid; also as taking part in a larger cosmic circuit, or in many larger circuits of magnetism or energy which flowed through him from the universe about him, thus renewing the vitality of his personality.

We find Mesmer constantly speaking both of increasing the rapidity of the flow of magnetism through the body and of equilibriating that vital flow. He does not care to speak of "charging" the patient with magnetism or of "saturating" him with the fluid. His theory consisted solely in the idea of *equilibriating* the disturbed vitality in the body of his patient.

Following Mesmer, we come to the Abbé Faria, a French priest who, after experimenting some time with mesmerism, announced in 1814 a view of the subject comparable to that held at this day. That is to say, he did not stress any actual communication or even equilibriation of magnetism from healer to patient as being the primary factor in therapy. He held the view that the effects were mainly subjective. The mesmeric state was possibly due to changes in the mind and body of the subject produced by faith and expectancy. In other words it was an anticipation on general lines of the later theory that the hypnotic or mesmeric state was induced solely by expectancy and by suggestion. At the time, however, this view was glossed over and forgotten.

Although at the date of Mesmer's death in 1815 his system of procedure of inducing a violent crisis in the patient was followed in its integrity by a considerable number of practitioners almost everywhere, more especially in Germany, there were already two other more or less important schools of Animal Magnetism in existence. One of these was the school of de Barbarin, who taught that the cures were effected directly through the providence of God, being in reality the result of faith alone. The processes of Mesmer, he held, served but to disguise that fact, and in no way to assist the cure which was in every instance produced by an "act of the soul". Having no new processes to describe, and no new worth-while theory to enunciate, this school has left very little record of its existence.

The development of Magnetism in the so-called "Experimental" school of the operators who were undoubtedly the legitimate heirs and successors of Mesmer, caused the disappearance of the schools both of Mesmer proper and of de Barbarin. But who were the "great magnetizers" of this experimental school ? These included a great many operators in almost every country in Europe. Many were physicians who, during the last quarter of the eighteenth century and the first quarter of the nineteenth, devoted themselves to magnetic therapy. Some established private institutions where patients were received, whilst others operated in various hospitals. The best known of that generation of magnetizers are the Marquis de Puységur, Baron du Potet, Deleuze, and Lafontaine, all of whom have left treatises on the subject. Very soon, de Puységur, as a pioneer, began to move away from his master both in the theory and practise of Magnetism. Indeed we may safely say that the later magnetizers followed the pupil rather than the master. Were we to call the processes of Mesmer and the violent effects in the artificial crisis which he encouraged as "Mesmerism" then the real discoverer of Animal Magnetism, as it has been known for the last hundred years, as a phenomenon rather than as a theory, is the Marquis de Puységur, the acknowledged founder of the "Experimental" school. It is to him that are due the processes now generally known as mesmeric—processes which are productive of results differing considerably from those produced by Mesmer himself. De Puységur's early instructions for magnetizing are as follows: "You are to consider yourself as a magnet; your arms and particularly your hands being its poles ; and when you touch a patient by laying one of your hands on his back, and the other in direct opposition upon his stomach, you are to imagine that the magnetic fluid has a tendency to circulate from one hand to the other through the body of the patient. You may vary this position by placing one hand on the head and the other on the stomach, still with the same intention, the same desire of doing good. The circulation from one hand to the other will continue, the head and stomach being the parts of the body where the greatest number of nerves converge ; these are, therefore, the two centres to which your action ought to be mostly directed. Friction is quite unnecessary ; it is sufficient to touch with great intention."

There was a fundamental difference between the theories of Mesmer and de Puységur. The former emphatically asserted that magnetism was an ccean of life and vitality permeating all things, and pervading the earth and the air as well as the human system. His conception of his cure by the magnetic technique was simply the adjustment of the disturbed flow of magnetic or etheric currents within the system of his patients. De Puységur, on the other hand, held the idea that the operator definitely imparts magnetism or vitality to the patient, and that such an imparting of power is responsible for the restoration of health. It is significant that neither Mesmer nor the adherents of his school ever complained of fatigue or exhaustion after treatments, whilst, on the other hand, it was no common thing for the practitioners of the experimental school to experience exhaustion after a certain number of treatments. The modern magical conception really combines both theories. Not only does it postulate as a categorical fact the existence of cosmic ethers or flows of vitality and spiritual power, but it carries the postulate a step further. These cosmic streams of force, pervading and permeating all space and all things therein, must of necessity permeate the physical and astral form of man. Thus within him are mirrored the forces of the cosmos ; he is a miniature epitome of the macrocosm. By the employment of his volitional and imaginative faculties, the intelligent man is able to direct these currents through his own physique, willing their entrance into the system of another for therapeutic or other purposes. It is only man's egotism and self-willed complacency that shuts off the free flow of the spirit. The libido flows up freely from the Unconscious when there are no resistances, the individual Unconscious receiving its power and its very existence from the Collective Unconscious— that which is common to all men and the whole of life.

De Puységur's first discovery of any importance was that in the drowsy or somnambulistic state which quite early is produced by the application of magnetism, it was possible to address the patient and obtain evidence of a very high order of intelligence. Mesmer was previously aware of the induction of somnambulism but rarely interfered with it, considering it as a natural state by means of which the system adjusted its inequilibrium. Dr. William Gregory, many years later, in describing the somnambulistic patient declares that his whole manner seems to undergo an improvement and refinement. "It would seem as if the brute or animal propensities were laid to rest, while the intellect and higher sentiments shone forth." What interested de Puységur most about this new discovery was that not only did the replies he received from sleeping patients show the most marvellous insight into their own symptoms and the means of treating them, but they gave evidence of the extraordinary phenomenon of telepathy. Here was the beginning of what came to be known as the "higher phenomena".

His second discovery was made in 1811. It consisted in finding out how to produce the somnambulistic state more quickly and more efficiently than before, namely by the use of passes. Several years later, du Potet laid more stress on the effect of the will and less on benevolent intentions, relying far more even than did de Puységur on the fixation of the eye and the passes. Lafontaine, who has been called the last of the great magnetizers, relied almost exclusively on the passes, except that sometimes he established contact with the hands while looking into the eyes of his subjects. Of course, his will was exerted powerfully all the time.

Chiefly responsible for introducing Mesmerism into England was Dr. John Elliotson, who employed it surgically at University College Hospital, London. No sooner had Elliotson demonstrated its efficiency—and he did that in a most remarkable way—than his medical colleagues commenced to deride and ridicule both him and his practice. The term hypnotism as a less objectionable and more scientific term for certain aspects of the mesmeric state was first coined in 1843 by a Manchester physician, Dr. James Braid. It was in 1842 that he first began experimental work with mesmerism, and seems to have been the first modern practitioner deliberately to use the technique of fixation of sight and suggestion instead of passes and the laying on of hands. Even the bright object was after a while eliminated, since in some patients it aggravated conjunctivitis, the entire stress being now laid upon verbal suggestion.

Another eminent pioneer was James Esdaile, a Scottish medico stationed in India. He appears to have been the first British mesmerist to receive some measure of official support. From 1845 onwards he employed mesmeric states for painless surgery with great success at various Indian hospitals, and the record of his operations by these means make thrilling reading. Many of his operations were for the

removal of monstrous scrotal tumours weighing nearly a
hundredweight, horrible but deadly convincing evidence of
the effectiveness of his technique. The discovery and wide
application of ether and chloroform for painless surgery
put an end to the interest in hypnotic experimental work.
From 1842 to more or less the end of the century there is a
break in the history of hypnotism in England. On the
Continent, however, we come across famous names like
Liébault, Bernheim, Moll, Charcot, Janet, and the beginning of different groups of hypnotic operators coming
to hold vastly different theories—the Nancy School, the
Salpétrière School, etc. Doctors Lloyd Tuckey, Morton
Prince, Vincent Wingfield, Milne Bramwell, and Bernard
Hollander, are other names of English experimentalists
who have done much to restore public confidence and
scientific respectability to the subject more recently.

Manifestly this is no more than a superficial glance
at the subject. It is only in an indirect way that we are
here concerned with animal magnetism as a therapeutic
agent. My reasons for this outline are that Mrs. Atwood,
whose theory I am to delineate and expand, held that the
practice of Mesmerism *might* be considered as the first step to
the solution of the alchemic mystery. That she had vast
insight and understanding is a statement which cannot be
doubted. Before she was yet thirty this astonishing young
woman wrote, at her father's instance, a small work entitled
*Early Magnetism, in its higher relations to Humanity as veiled
in the Poets and the Prophets.* Written in 1846 when most
other mesmerists and hypnotists were engaged solely in
therapeutic work or in the application of the trance state
to the production of psychic phenomena such as clairvoyance
and telepathy, etc., this woman and her father, Mr. South,
were displaying an acumen and insight which are literally
amazing. They realized other and more spiritual possibilities
concealed within the practice of animal magnetism. In this
work she expressed the view that in its application to
higher ideals, one object of the magnetic trance might be
to conjoin the mind to its lost spiritual universality. She
believed it might be possible to pass the consciousness
regressively through its many phases of historical evolutionary development back to the long-forgotten life in Reality,

"passing behind the murky media of sense and fantasy to behold reflected in the brightened mirror of our own intelligence the pure Truth ; not as it may appear individually or arbitrarily but in its characteristic necessity and universality".

Furthermore, in describing the technique to be pursued, she adds :

> The trance state when justly and perseveringly ordered for that end, affords the metaphysical condition pre-eminently perfect; for it removes the sensible obstruction and presents a clearer glass before the mind than it can ever regard in the natural state. The patient is no sooner lightly entranced than he begins to feel an internality never before known to him and which may be intensified as the intention is fixed and the calibre of the mind and circumstantial conditions are favourable ; the passive personality collapses from its circumferential and phenomenal life into that central Omnipresence whose circumference is not ; whilst the mind, rightly disciplined and related to the Universal becomes universalized and one with the great magnetic Will of Nature, revolving with the Infinite Medium (the pure ether) through all its spheres, perceiving all things in all and in itself, until at length becoming perfectly converted to its principle, the divinized microcosmic epitome moves with demiurgic power and grace.

Here we have a mystical and religious conception which so far transcends the previous practice of magnetism as, for example, the Jungian concept of psychotherapy transcends the cruder and pioneer theories of the Freudian school. For whatever may or may not have been the underlying ground of belief and procedure in the alchemical writings, at any rate Mrs. Atwood's hypothesis is so suggestive and far-reaching in its practical implications that one hesitates considerably to discard it without having subjected it thoroughly to a critical test.

Although the alchemists were firm and adamant in their instruction that nothing could be accomplished without the preliminary dissolution, they have left but little clue as to the significance of this operation. It is true that they have spoken of manual operations, but it seems that this could lend countenance not only to the mesmeric passes but also to the physical and metallurgical theory where transmutation was accomplished or attempted by hard labour and by sweat of the brow. The first way of approach and the closed entrance to these manual operations remained a mystery, and its secret if we except this thesis had not yet been unfolded. Nor, if we may accept the admonition contained in their own writings, would it be possible to discover the method from a cursory examination of their books alone. Yet the process itself, as a technical method always must be, is said to have been in itself a very simple one. For it is called by some of them a play of children and is represented as very trivial, slight, almost a ridiculous thing.

Recent observation, or rather experience, during the last one hundred years or so, has elicited various means of discovering this secret. The enormous progress which has been made in the translation of obscure Eastern texts dealing with the art of meditation, concentration, and religious exaltation, give us several clues. In fact, one modern alchemical apologist claims that the secret lies in a species of meditation and introversion leading to a self-induced trance state in which consciousness as such is not obscured, as for example it is in certain spiritualistic trance states. On the contrary, it is claimed that consciousness becomes heightened and exalted by these methods, and all the faculties of mind are sharpened and left in a much stronger condition than before. Not only so, but that the ego is much more able to deal with life and living than ever it was prior to having undertaken this particular type of psychic training.

The psychological method, which previously we examined, is also another and very effective method. Its popularity and the increasing interest in its technique is proof of the hold which it has taken in the popular mind not only as a means of therapy but as a philosophical mode of self-discovery and knowledge.

But the trance state as induced by magnetism and the reactions induced in the subject are so suggestive over and above these other symptoms that we are tempted to wonder whether here is not some technical method which answers to the enigmatical descriptions left to us by the ancients. We know full well that some magnetic method of entrancement was widely practised in Greece. Thousands of years ago the Phrygian Dactyli, the initiated priests, spoken of as the magicians and exorcists of sickness, healed disease by these processes. These methods were the principal agents in theurgic mysteries as also in the Aesculapiea—the healing Temples of Aesculapius, where the patients were treated during the process of "incubation", as it was termed, magnetically in sleep.

Certain of Mr. Arthur Edward Waite's criticisms to the Atwood theory in his work *The Secret Tradition in Alchemy* demand some attention here. It would be difficult to find anywhere such unnecessary controversial criticism as is found in Mr. Waite's book. For one thing he accuses her of employing a turgid, difficult style. This is certainly true. But the psychological mechanism of projection must operate here, for Mr. Waite's style is hardly beyond criticism in these very respects. However, it is not to the literary aspect of his criticisms that attention need be called at length. He remarks towards the end of his book that

> it is of common knowledge that the psychic state of many entranced subjects conveyed an impression of purity, refinement, beauty, as if the actual or comparative grosser part has been put to sleep for the time being. But this state is as far removed from the spiritual attainment envisaged by Platonic successors as are the records of trance mediumship from the realizations of Eckhart and Ruysbroeck, speaking in the light of the union.

Why Mr. Waite should utter this criticism against the Atwood hypothesis, it is hard to realize. It is particularly out of place, for the point he raises is precisely the argument of Mrs. Atwood. She argues that if we compare the first effects of mesmerism, that is the somnambulistic state in which the so-called higher phenomena of community of sense and feeling manifest, with the sacred art of the ancients, the former appears but trivial. The supreme spiritual wisdom attained in divine union, the self-knowledge the ancients desired and the perfection of life and immortality their system promised and said to have been bestowed on those initiated into the higher mysteries, these are objects quite outside of the vision of the mesmerists. What has Mesmerism to do with spiritual ends such as these? What is its philosophy, she asked? Has it yet attempted to investigate consciousness and its deeps and origins? Naturally, the ordinary mesmeric state bore no resemblance to the sublime mystic state of the great saints and philosophers. And it is her hypothesis that this was realized by and known to the alchemists who employed magnetism *only* as the first step towards the consummation of the divine mystery. It was by this means that the hermetic solution was accomplished. From this the other steps could be perceived and climbed. To effect this solution was only the *beginning* of the Hermetic art.

The medium (that is the astro-mental sheath) in its natural state is volatile, immanifest, fantastic, irrational and impotent, compared with what it subsequently is able and by artificial conception suffers itself to become. The Alchemists, we repeat therefore, did not remain satisfied with a few passes of the hand or any first phenomena whatever, but they proceeded at once scientifically to purify, depriving the ether of its wild affections and impressures by a dissolution of the circulating body in its own blood. For this is the brazen Wall celebrated by Antiquity. Take the occult Nature, which is our Brass, says Albertus, and wash it that it may be pure and clean.

Thus it is seen that the strictures of Mr. Waite are wholly without foundation. And I confess to a sense of sad disappointment in him. The Atwood theory of mesmerism as applied to the Hermetic mystery is, in my opinion, so important and so suggestive that it may be well to quote from her work at greater length in order to clarify exactly what it is that she proposes. When commenting upon *The Six Keys of Eudoxus* I shall attempt to dilate upon this theory, simplifying her terminology and employing the comparative method.

First of all it was her belief that there was a secret con-
nected with the Mystery celebrations of the ancients which
no modern so-called intellectual criticism has explained away
or divulged.

A few writers on Animal Magnetism [she notes],
having within these few years become enlightened by
that singular discovery, suggest their Trance and its
phenomena as a revelation of the Temple Mysteries and
various religious rites. But no one, that we are aware,
has developed this suggestion or carried the idea sufficiently above the therapeutic sphere ; they appear to have
taken a broad view, without particular inquiry into the
nature of the rites from the ancients themselves. Had they
done this (we speak of the more advanced minds) we are
persuaded that with that key in hand, their attention
would have been drawn in new directions and their
satisfaction about the modern use of it become much
modified by observing the far superior results which
through their Theurgic disciplines, the ancients aspired
after, different too, as they were superior to any that we
are accustomed to imagine even at the present day.

The ordinary effects of Animal Magnetism, or Mesmerism, or vital Magnetism, or by whatever other term the
unknown agency is better expressed, are now so familiarly
known in practice that it will be unnecessary to describe
them ; they have attracted the attention of the best and
leading minds of the present age, who have hailed with
admiration a discovery which enables man to alleviate
pain and maladies insurmountable by other means. . . .
But years have passed and the science has not grown, but
retrograded rather in interest and power, since de
Mainaduc, Puységur, Colquhoun, Elliotson, Townsend,
Dupotet, and the rest, faithful spirits, first set their fellow
men on the road of inquiry.

Her position and her attitude to the history and theory
of Magnetism is thus made crystal clear ; no possibility
exists for misunderstanding. The hypothesis which she came
to adopt did not stop with the acceptance of the psychical
phenomena produced by the practice of the mesmeric art.

A pioneer in an intellectual world, and a woman with a clearer spiritual vision and foresight than most of her day, she realized the intrinsically invaluable nature of the technique. She perceived that the experimental work of therapy and investigation of the higher phenomena was interesting and intriguing no doubt, but clearly it was not the sort of investigation that the ancients followed in their mysteries. It is true that they worked on the same kind of material, with similar instruments, and with a similar technical method. Yet their practice was different, because it was conducted upon established philosophical principles and with a truly enlightened as well as benevolent aim. That Mesmerism affords entrance together with the imagination into another kind of consciousness was the contention she could not doubt.

And more than this, in well-conditioned cases, we have proof of the intrinsical intelligence and power of the Free Spirit which can expatiate into the whole circumference of its sphere and reveal hidden things, exhibiting a variety of gifts. . . . This Mesmerism, in respect of our Mystery then, may be regarded as a first key which, opening into the vestibule, affords a view within the sense's prison, but of the labyrinth of life only.

These protracted quotations will provide some preliminary notion as to what manner this practice of Magnetism is conceived of in this hypothesis. It is obvious that Mrs. Atwood regards it solely as an elementary view of a diviner state of consciousness, as the entrance into the hermetic mystery, solely as a means of entry and nothing more. Beyond this first stage, other means are to be employed, other techniques—a utilization of the magnetic art to transcend itself into perfection. This idea will expand itself as we read and examine the text following, and I shall attempt to dilate upon the simpler aspects of the technique in a brief commentary.

CHAPTER SIX

*The Six Keys of Eudoxus, opening into the most Secret Philosophy.**

THE FIRST KEY

1. The First Key is that which opens the dark prisons in which the Sulphur is shut up : this is it which knows how to extract the seed out of the body, and which forms the Stone of the philosophers by the conjunction of the spirit with the body—of sulphur with mercury.

2. Hermes has manifestly demonstrated the operation of this First Key by these words : In the caverns of the metals there is hidden the Stone, which is venerable, bright in colour, a mind sublime, and an open sea.

3. This Stone has a bright glittering : it contains a Spirit of a sublime original ; it is the Sea of the Wise, in which they angle for their mysterious Fish.

4. But the operations of the three works have a great deal of analogy one to another, and the philosophers do designedly speak in equivocal terms, to the end that those who have not the Lynx's eyes may pursue wrong, and be lost in this labyrinth, from whence it is very hard to get out. In effect, when one imagines that they speak of one work, they often treat of another.

5. Take heed, therefore, not to be deceived here ; for it is a truth, that in each work the Wise Artist ought to dissolve the body with the spirit ; he must cut off the Raven's head, whiten the Black, and vivify the White ; yet it is properly in the First operation that the Wise Artist cuts off the head of the Black Dragon and of the Raven.

---

*This text I have reproduced from Mrs. Atwood's book. She has taken it from *The Hermetical Triumph* by A. T. Limojonde St. Didier. This latter was translated from French into English in 1723. Mrs. Atwood has altered some of the wording in certain respects. I have again introduced numbering of the versicles for convenience' sake.

6. Hence, Hermes says, What is born of the Crow is the beginning of this Art. Consider that it is by separation of the black, foul, and stinking fume of the Blackest Black that our astral, white, and resplendent Stone is formed, which contains in its veins the blood of the Pelican. It is at this First Purification of the Stone, and at this shining whiteness, that the work of the First Key is ended.

THE SECOND KEY

1. The Second Key dissolves the compound of the Stone, and begins the separation of the Elements in a philosophical manner : this separation of the elements is not made but by raising up the subtle and pure parts above the thick and terrestrial parts.

2. He who knows how to sublime the Stone philosophically, justly deserves the name of a philosopher, since he knows *the Fire of the Wise*, which is the *only instrument* which can work this sublimation. No philosopher has ever openly revealed this Secret Fire, and this powerful agent, which works all the wonders of the Art : he who shall not understand it, and not know how to distinguish it by the characters whereby it is described, ought to make a stand here, and pray to God to make it clear to him ; for the knowledge of this great Secret is rather a gift of Heaven, than a Light acquired by the natural force of reasoning ; let him, nevertheless, read the writings of the philosophers ; let him meditate ; and, above all, let him pray : there is no difficulty which may not in the end be made clear by Work, Meditation, and Prayer.

3. Without the sublimation of the Stone, the conversion of the Elements and the extraction of the Principles is impossible ; and this conversion, which makes Water of Earth, Air of Water, and Fire of Air, is the only way whereby our Mercury can be prepared.

4. Apply yourself then to know this Secret Fire, which dissolves the Stone naturally and without violence, and makes it dissolve into Water in the great sea of the Wise, *by the distillation which is made by the rays of the Sun and Moon.*

5. It is in this manner that the Stone, which, according

to Hermes, is the vine of the Wise, becomes their Wine,
which, by the operations of Art, produces their rectified
Water of Life, and their most sharp Vinegar. The Elements
of the Stone cannot be dissolved but by this Nature wholly
Divine ; nor can a perfect dissolution be made of it, but after
a proportioned digestion and putrefaction, at which the
operation of the Second Key of the First Work is ended.

The Third Key

1. The Third Key comprehends of itself alone a longer
train of operations than all the rest together. The philosophers have spoken very little of it, seeing the Perfection
of our *Mercury* depends thereon ; the sincerest even, as
Artefius, Trevisan, Flammel, have passed in silence the
Preparation of our Mercury, and there is hardly one
found who has not feigned, instead of showing the longest
and the most important of the operations of our Practice.
With a design to lend you a hand in this part of the way,
which you have to go, and where for want of Light it is
impossible to know the true road, I will enlarge myself
more than others have done on this Third Key ; or at least
I will follow in an order, that which they have treated so
confusedly, that without the inspiration of Heaven, or without the help of a faithful friend, one remains undoubtedly in
this labyrinth, without being able to find a happy deliver-
ance from thence.

2. I am sure, that you who are the true Sons of Science
will receive a very great satisfaction in the explaining of these
hidden Mysteries, which regard the separation and the purification of the *Principles of our Mercury*, which is made by a
perfect dissolution and glorification of the body, whence it
had its nativity, and by the intimate union of the soul with
its body, of whom the Spirit is the only tie which works this
conjunction.

3. This is the *Intention*, and the essential point of the
Operations of this Key, which terminate at the generation
of a new substance infinitely nobler than the First.

4. After the Wise Artist has made a spring of living water
come out of the stone, and has pressed out the vine of the

philosophers, and has made their wine, he ought to take
notice that in this homogeneous substance, which appears
under the form of Water, there are three different substances, and three natural principles of bodies—Salt, Sulphur
and Mercury—which are the spirit, the soul, and the body ;
and though they appear pure and perfectly united together,
there still wants much of their being so ; for *when by distillation
we draw the Water, which is the soul and the spirit, the Body
remains in the bottom of the vessel*, like a dead, black, and dreggy
earth, which, nevertheless, is not to be despised ; for in our
subject there is nothing which is not good.

5. The philosopher, John Pontanus, protests that the
very superfluities of the Stone are converted into a true
essence, and that he who pretends to separate anything from
our subject knows nothing of philosophy ; for that all which
is therein superfluous, unclean, dreggy—in fine, the whole
compound, is made perfect by the action of our Fire.

6. This advice opens the eyes of those, who, to make an
exact purification of the Elements and of the Principles,
persuade themselves that they must only take the subtile
and cast away the heavy. But Hermes says the power of it
is not integral until it be turned into earth ; neither ought the
sons of science to be ignorant that the Fire and the Sulphur
are hidden in the centre of the *Earth*, and that they must wash
it exactly with its spirit, to extract out of it the *Fixed Salt*,
which is the Blood of our Stone. This is the essential Mystery
of the operation, which is not accomplished till after a
convenient digestion and a slow distillation.

7. You know that nothing is more contrary than fire and
water ; but yet the Wise Artist must make peace between
the enemies, who radically love each other vehemently.
Cosmopolite told the manner thereof in a few words : All
things therefore being purged make Fire and Water to be
Friends, which they will easily do in their earth, which
had ascended with them. Be then attentive on this point ;
moisten oftentimes the earth with its water, and you will
obtain what you seek. Must not the body be dissolved by
the water, and the Earth be penetrated with its Humidity,
to be made proper for generation ? According to philosophers, the Spirit is Eve, the Body is Adam ; they ought to be
joined together for the propagation of their species. Hermes

says the same in other terms : "For Water is the strongest Nature which surmounts and excites the fixed Nature in the Body, that is, rejoices in it."

8. In effect, these two substances, which are of the same nature but of different genders, ascend insensibly together, leaving but a little fæces in the bottom of their vessel ; so that the soul, spirit, and body, after an exact purification, appear at last inseparably united under a more noble and more perfect Form than it was before, and as different from its first liquid Form as the alcohol of Wine exactly rectified and actuated with its salt is different from the substance of the wine from whence it has been drawn ; this comparison is not only very fitting, but it furthermore gives the sons of science a precise knowledge of the operations of the Third Key.

9. Our Water is a living Spring which comes out of the Stone by a natural miracle of our philosophy. The first of all is the water which issueth out of this Stone. It is Hermes who has pronounced this great Truth. He acknowledges, further, that this water is the foundation of our Art.

10. The philosophers give it many names ; for sometimes they call it wine, sometimes water of life, sometimes vinegar, sometimes oil, according to the different degrees of Preparation, or according to the diverse effects which it is capable of producing.

11. Yet I let you know that it is properly called the Vinegar of the Wise, and that in the distillation of this Divine Liquor there happens the same thing as in that of common vinegar ; you may hence draw instruction : the water and the phlegm ascend first ; the oily substance, in which the efficacy of the water consists, comes the last, etc.

12. It is therefore necessary to dissolve the body entirely to extract all its humidity which contains the precious ferment, the sulphur, that balm of Nature, and wonderful unguent, without which you ought not to hope ever to see in your vessel this blackness so desired by all the philosophers. Reduce then the whole compound into water, and make a perfect union of the volatile with the fixed ; it is a precept of Senior's, which deserves attention, that the highest fume should be reduced to the lowest ; for the divine water is the thing descending from heaven, the reducer of the soul to its body, which it at length revives.

13. The Balm of Life is hid in these unclean fæces ; you ought to wash them with this cœlestial water until you have removed away the blackness from them, and then your Water shall be animated with this Fiery Essence, which works all the wonders of our Art.

14. But, further, that you may not be deceived with the terms of the Compound, I will tell you that the philosophers have two sorts of compounds. The first is the compound of Nature, wherof I have spoken in the First Key ; for it is Nature which makes it in a manner incomprehensible to the Artist, who does nothing but lend a hand to Nature by the adhibition of external things, by the means of which she brings forth and produces this admirable compound.

15. The second is the compound of Art ; it is the *Wise* man who makes it by the secret union of the fixed with the volatile, perfectly conjoined with all prudence, which cannot be acquired but by the lights of a profound philosophy.

16. The compound of Art is not altogether the same in the Second as in the Third Work ; yet it is always the Artist who makes it. Geber defines it, a mixture of Argent vive and Sulphur, that is to say, of the volatile and the fixed ; which, acting on one another, are volatilized and fixed reciprocally into a perfect Fixity. Consider the example of Nature ; you see that the earth will never produce fruit if it be not penetrated with its humidity, and that the humidity would always remain barren if it were not retained and fixed by the dryness of the earth.

17. So, in the Art, you can have no success if you do not in the first work purify the Serpent, born of the Slime of the earth ; if you do not whiten these foul and black fæces, to separate from thence the white sulphur, which is the Sal Amoniac of the Wise, and their Chaste Diana, who washes herself in the bath ; and all this mystery is but the extraction of the *fixed salt* of our compound, in which the whole *energy* of our Mercury consists.

18. The water which ascends by distillation carries up with it a part of this fiery salt, so that the affusion of the water on the body, reiterated many times, impregnates, fattens, and fertilizes our Mercury, and makes it fit to be fixed, which is the end of the second Work.

19. One cannot better explain this Truth than by Hermes, in these words :

> When I saw that the water by degrees did become thicker and harder I did rejoice, for I certainly knew that I should find what I sought for.

It is not without reason that the philosophers give this viscous Liquor the name of Pontick Water. Its exuberant ponticity is indeed the true character of its virtue, and the more you shall rectify it, and the more you shall work upon it, the more virtue will it acquire. It has been called the Water of Life, because it gives life to the metals ; but it is properly called the great Lunaria, because of its brightness wherewith it shines. . . .

20. Since I speak only to you, ye true scholars of Hermes, I will reveal to you one secret which you will not find entirely in the books of the philosophers. Some of them say, that of their liquor they make two Mercuries—the one White and the other Red ; Flammel has said more particularly, that one must make use of the citrine Mercury to make the Imbibition to the Red ; giving notice to the Sons of Art not to be deceived on this point, as he himself had been, unless the Jew had informed him of the truth.

21. Others have taught that the White Mercury is the bath of the Moon, and that the Red Mercury is the bath of the Sun. But there are none who have been willing to show distinctly to the Sons of Science by what means they may get these two mercuries. If you apprehend me well, you have the point already cleared up to you.

22. The Lunaria is the White Mercury, the most sharp Vinegar is the Red Mercury ; but the better to *determine* these two mercuries, feed them with flesh of their own species—the blood of innocents whose throats are cut ; that is to say, the spirits of the bodies are the Bath where the Sun and Moon go to wash themselves.

23. I have unfolded to you a great mystery, if you reflect well on it ; the philosophers who have spoken thereof have passed over this important point very slightly. Cosmopolite has very wittily mentioned it by an ingenious allegory, speaking of the purification of the Mercury : This will be

done, says he, if you shall give our old man gold and silver to swallow, that he may consume them, and at length he also dying may be burnt. He makes an end of describing the whole magistery in these terms : Let his ashes be strewed in the water ; boil it until it is enough, and you have a medicine to cure the leprosy. You must not be ignorant that Our Old Man is our Mercury ; this name indeed agrees with him because He is the first matter of all metals. He is their water, as the same author goes on to say, and to which he gives also the name of steel and of the lodestone ; adding for a greater confirmation of what I am about to discover to you, that if gold couples with it eleven times it sends forth its seed, and is debilitated almost unto death ; but the Chalybes conceives and begets a son more glorious than the Father.

24. Behold a great Mystery which I reveal to you without an enigma ; this is the secret of the two mercuries which contain the two tinctures. Keep them separately, and do not confound their species, for fear they should beget a monstrous Lineage.

25. I not only speak to you more intelligibly than any philosopher before has done, but I also reveal to you the most essential point in the Practice ; if you meditate thereon, and apply yourself to understand it well ; but above all, if you work according to those lights which I give you, you may obtain what you seek for.

26. And if you come not to these knowledges by the way which I have pointed out to you, I am very well assured that you will hardly arrive at your design by only reading the philosophers. Therefore despair of nothing—search the source of the Liquor of the Sages, which contains all that is necessary for the work ; it is hidden under the Stone—strike upon it with the Red of Magic Fire, and a clear fountain will issue out ; then do as I have shown you, prepare the bath of the King with the blood of the Innocents, and you will have the animated Mercury of the wise, which never loses its virtue, if you keep it in a vessel well closed.

27. Hermes says, that there is so much sympathy between the purified bodies and the spirits, that they never quit one another when they are united together : because this union resembles that of the soul with the glorified body ; after which Faith tells us, there shall be no more separation or death ;

because the spirits desire to be in the cleansed bodies, and having them, they enliven and dwell in them.

28. By this you may observe the merit of this precious liquor, to which the philosophers have given more than a thousand different names, which is in sum the great Alcahest, which radically dissolves the metals—a true permanent water which, after having radically dissolved them, is inseparably united to them, increasing their weight and tincture.

THE FOURTH KEY

The Fourth Key of the Art is the entrance to the Second Work (and a reiteration in part and development of the foregoing) : it is this which reduces our Water into Earth ; there is but this only Water in the world, which by a bare boiling can be converted into Earth, because the Mercury of the Wise carries in its centre its own Sulphur, which coagulates it. The terrification of the Spirit is the only operation of this work. Boil them with patience ; if you have proceeded well, you will not be a long time without perceiving the marks of this coagulation ; and if they appear not in their time, they will never appear ; because it is an undoubted sign that you have failed in some essential thing in the former operations ; for to corporify the Spirit, which is our Mercury, you must have well dissolved the body in which the Sulphur which coagulates the Mercury is enclosed. But Hermes assumes that our mercurial water shall obtain all the virtues which the philosophers attribute to it if it be turned into earth. An earth admirable is it for fertility—the Land of Promise of the Wise, who, knowing how to make the dew of Heaven fall upon it, cause it to produce fruits of an inestimable price. Cultivate then diligently this precious earth, moisten it often with its own humidity, dry it as often, and you will no less augment its virtue than its weight and its fertility.

THE FIFTH KEY

The Fifth Key includes the Fermentation of the Stone with the perfect body, to make thereof the medicine of the

H

Third order. I will say nothing in particular of the operation of the Third work ; except that the Perfect Body is a
necessary leaven of Our Paste. And that the Spirit ought to
make the union of the paste with the leaven in the same
manner as water moistens meal, and dissolves the leaven
to compose a fermented paste fit to make bread. This comparison is very proper ; Hermes first made it, saying, that as
a paste cannot be fermented without a ferment ; so when
you shall have sublimed, cleansed and separated the foulness
from the Fæces, and would make the conjunction, put a
ferment to them and make the water earth, that the paste
may be made a ferment ; which repeats the instruction of
the whole work, and shows, that just so as the whole lump
of the paste becomes leaven, by the action of the ferment
which has been added, so all the philosophic confection
becomes, by this operation, a leaven proper to ferment a
new matter, and to multiply it to infinity. If you observe
well how bread is made, you will find the *proportions also*,
which you ought to keep among the matters which compose
our philosophical paste. Do not the bakers put more meal
than leaven, and more water than the leaven and the meal ?
The laws of Nature are the rules you ought to follow in the
practice of our magistery. I have given you, upon the principal point, all the instructions which are necessary for you, so
that it would be superfluous to tell you more of it ; particularly concerning the last operations, about which the Adepts
have been less reserved than at the First, which are the
foundations of the Art.

THE SIXTH KEY

The Sixth Key teaches the Multiplication of the Stone,
by the reiteration of the same operation, which consists but
in opening and shutting, dissolving and coagulating, imbib-
ing and drying ; whereby the virtues of the Stone are infinitely augmentable. As my design has been not to describe
entirely the application of the three medicines, but only to
instruct you in the more important operations concerning the
preparation of Mercury, which the philosophers commonly pass over in silence, to hide the mysteries from the

profane which are only intended for the wise, I will tarry
no longer upon this point, and will tell you nothing more of
what relates to the Projection of the Medicine, because the
success you expect depends not thereon. I have not given
you very full instructions except on the Third Key, because
it contains a long train of operations which, though simple
and natural, require a great understanding of the Laws of
Nature, and of the qualities of Our Matter, as well as a perfect knowledge of chemistry and of the different degrees of
heat which are fitting for these operations. I have conducted you by the straight way without any winding ; and
if you have well minded the road which I have pointed out
to you, I am sure that you will go straight to the end without
straying. Take this in good part from me, in the design which
I had of sparing you a thousand labours and a thousand
troubles, which I myself have undergone in this painful
journey for want of an assistance such as this is, which I
give you from a sincere heart and a tender affection for all
the true sons of science. I should much bewail, if, like me,
after having known the true matter, you should spend fifteen
years entirely in the work, in study and in meditation,
without being able to extract out of the Stone the precious
juice which it encloses in its bosom, for want of knowing the
secret fire of the wise, which makes to run out of this plant
(dry and withered in appearance) a water which wets not
the hands, and which by a magical union of the dry water
of the sea of the wise, is dissolved into a viscous water—into
a mercurial liquor, which is the beginning, the foundation,
and the Key of our Art : Convert, separate, and purify the
elements, as I have taught you, and you will possess the
true Mercury of the philosophers, which will give you the
fixed Sulphur and the Universal Medicine. But I give you
notice, moreover, that even after you shall be arrived at the
knowledge of the Secret Fire of the Wise, yet still you shall
not attain your point at your first career. I have erred many
years in the way which remains to be gone, to arrive at the
mysterious fountain where the King bathes himself, is made
young again, and retakes a new life exempt from all sorts of
infirmities. Besides this you must know how to purify, to
heal, and to animate the royal bath ; it is to lend you a hand
in this secret way that I have expatiated under the Third

Key, where all those operations are described. I wish with all my heart that the instructions which I have given you may enable you to go directly to the End. But remember, ye sons of philosophy, that the knowledge of our Magistery comes rather by the Inspiration of Heaven than from the Lights which we can get by ourselves. This truth is acknowledged by all artists ; it is for this reason that it is not enough to work; pray daily, read good books, and meditate night and day on the operations of Nature, and on what she may be able to do when she is assisted by the help of our Art ; and by these means you will succeed without doubt in your undertaking. This is all I have now to say to you. I was not willing to make you such a long discourse as the matter seemed to demand ; neither have I told you anything but what is essential to our Art ; so that if you know the Stone which is the only matter of Our Stone, and if you have the Understanding of Our Fire, which is both secret and natural, you have the Keys of the Art, and you can calcine Our Stone ; not by the common calcination which is made by the violence of fire, but by a philosophic calcination which is purely natural. Yet observe this, with the most enlightened philosophers, that there is this difference between the common calcination which is made by the force of Fire and the natural calcination ; that the first destroys the body and consumes the greatest part of its radical humidity ; but the second does not only preserve the humidity of the body in calcining it, but still considerably augments it. Experience will give you knowledge in the Practice of this great truth, for you will in effect find that this philosophical calcination, which sublimes and distils the Stone in calcining it, much augments its humidity; the reason is that the igneous spirit of the natural fire is corporified in the substances which are analogous to it. Our stone is an Astral Fire which sympathizes with the Natural Fire, and which, as a true Salamander receives its nativity, is nourished and grows in the Elementary Fire, which is geometrically proportioned to it.

CHAPTER SEVEN

AT the outset the text informs us that the object of this first key is triple. That is, it opens up (*a*) the dark prisons in which the Sulphur or the Fire, that is the emotional life or vital magnetism or prana, is confined. (*b*) The Seed is the philosophic Salt, the opposite of the Sulphur on the Qabalistic Tree, that Salt which, when purified, serves as the vehicular foundation of the enlightened mind, or the seed from which the Aurific Stone is formed. (*c*) It forms the Stone by the conjunction of the Sulphur and Mercury.

Clearly, the Stone represents the union of Mercury, which is Consciousness, and Sulphur, the fire of emotion, the *anima* principle of the psyche, using Salt as their basis of action, the astro-mental sheath. The psychological interpretation in its theoretical aspect is still applicable here. As in the former commentary, the analytical method may be employed to induce the dissolution of consciousness in its own light ; that is to say, by immersing its contents in that from which it originally issued, in the Unconscious. According to the magnetic theory, the approach to the first alchemical stage of dissolution is by means of the magnetic trance. Because of the transmission of great vitality from a skilled and initiated operator, consciousness suffers an eclipse, enabling the secondary consciousness, or the divine core of the Unconscious, to hold unrestricted expression. Exactly what occurs to consciousness during hypnosis or mesmerism remains even to this day a moot point. Some hold one view, others another. In Dr. Milne Bramwell's book on hypnotism, some hundred pages or so are taken up in a consideration of the various opinions as to the true state of consciousness. A footnote by Mrs. Atwood in her *Suggestive Inquiry into the Hermetic Mystery* expresses the following opinion :

We adopt the term *dissolve* here in accordance with the old doctrine ; varying theories have been proposed to explain the change that takes place in the vital relationship of the patient in the mesmeric trance ; some have thought the sensible medium is drawn away by a superior attraction of life in the agent ; others, that it is overcome, or included, or arrested, or destroyed ; but the Alchemists, with one accord, say it ought to be *dissolved* ; and, in default of better authority, shall we not suppose it so to be dissolved, or that it ought to be, the alkali by the acid, the dark dominion of the selfhood by the magnetic friction of its proper light, the sensible or animal into the vegetable, the cerebral into the ganglionic life ? *Corpora qui vult purgare oportet flux facere*, says the author of the Rosarium, that the compact earthy body of sense may be rarefied and flow as a passive watery spirit. The beginning of the work, says Albertus Magnus, is a perfect solution ; and all those that we teach is nothing else but to dissolve and recongeal the spirit, to make the fixed volatile and the volatile fixed, until the total nature is perfected by the reiteration, both in its Solary and Lunar form.

2. The compound of metals, or the aggregate of the astrological planets, with which the *Sephiros* of the Qabalistic Tree of Life and the metals are in correspondence, is the constitution of man. "Cavern" in symbolism quite frequently stands for the darkness of the bodily life, the womb and the dark creative interior of the Mother. Hence it is a generic universal symbol for the Unconscious itself, since it is from the vital dynamic urges and the inchoate mass of instincts that the conscious faculties gradually issue and evolve in the course of millions of years of evolution. The cave denotes an interior state or condition from which external things issue, or from which they are born—as in the case of the conscious intellectual life. In the Unconscious, then, are we to seek for the hidden Stone of the Wise. Our text affirms the speculation that every state of consciousness has associated with it, or functions in, a vehicle of substance of some kind. The Stone clearly represents the brilliant self-shining aura, the luminous emanation from the inner Body

of Light, glittering like some rare and precious jewel. In its proper sense the Stone is the term used to denote the unity of the Aura or astro-mental sheath, the vital magnetism or pranic energy of the individuality, the vital spirit so-called, and the central core of consciousness itself. The latter is concealed within the depths of man. Its antecedents go back to the very beginnings of evolution in the dim hazy epochs of primeval times ; thus it is venerable and sublime in nature. Eudoxus identifies it with the Collective Unconscious, the Sea of the Wise, using this term in its highest, widest, and all-inclusive sense as before implied. It is not only the psychic realm of the instincts, but also of the archetypal world of the higher faculties of discrimination, intuition, and spiritual wisdom and inspiration. For the instincts are but the reflection of the higher spiritual parts of the divine nature.

"Their mysterious Fish" ! What an intriguing expression ! It has its correspondences in the spermatozoon swimming in the seminal sea ; in the foetus bathed in the intra-uterine amniotic fluid. It symbolizes the possibility of life, points to the realm of the future and great promise, and belongs to that class of eloquent symbols depicting rebirth and regeneration. In this connection there is an interesting illustration in *The Book of Lambspring*, one of the several books of the *Hermetic Museum* translated by Waite. It shows two fish swimming in a sea. Over the illustration we read "Be warned and understand truly that two fishes are swimming in our Sea. The Sea is the body, the two fishes are Soul and Spirit". The text accompanying the picture is as follows :

> The sages will tell you
> That two fishes are in our sea
> Without any flesh or bones.
> Let them be cooked in their own water ;
> Then they also will become a vast sea,
> The vastness of which no man can describe.
> Moreover, the Sages say
> That the two fishes are one, not two ;
> They are two, and nevertheless they are one,
> Body, Spirit and Soul.
> Now I tell you most truly,
> Cook these three together

That there may be a very large sea.
Cook the sulphur with the sulphur,
And hold your tongue about it ;
Conceal your knowledge to your own advantage,
And you shall be free from poverty.
Only let your discovery remain a close secret.

We are now brought to the central definition of Alchemy, that it is the science of regeneration, of fermenting the individual consciousness so that it soars to its own high root of perfection.

The word *fermentation* conveys an idea of the perfecting principle and of the possibility of transmutation beyond any other word, and also of the fixation or everlasting preservation of which they speak (explains Mrs. Atwood) ; and so of immortality, it is the best image of the Divine Art which earthly processes give. Alchemy is a process of fermenting the vital spirit in and by its own light. The vital light is in the Universal as well as in the individual. In the Art the Individual draws the Universal.

5. In each operation are certain implicits. The previously held confused, and automatic intellectual concepts, those which have helped to crystallize consciousness and the emotional nature into a rigid and repressed entity, are to be broken down by a process of dissolution. The Raven must be decapitated. The root of evil, of imperfection and confusion lying latent in consciousness—that which primarily caused the inhibition of emotion, and the compulsive motivation of the mind by the repression mechanism—must be uncovered and recognized. Its clear recognition is in itself an act of destruction. For no man, unless he be psychically compelled or bound by folly and utterly without volition or common sense, will persist in a course of action which he knows will lead to his final destruction. With recognition comes an abreaction of the complex and a release of pent-up emotion and spiritual energy.

There is yet another sense in which this idea may be interpreted. As spirit is always in all systems of symbolism considered to be white in colour, pure in nature, and

COMMENTARY   121

ubiquitous in its operation, so its opposite, the body and the personality, is symbolized by the colour black. By the decapitation of the Raven, a black bird, enjoined by Eudoxus, is meant a separation in understanding (thus the name of Alchemy, the Spagyric or separative art) of the head—the higher spiritual and intellectual principles—from the lower part of the body, the world of conflicting desires and instincts. In *Splendor Solis*, by Solomon Trismosin, there is a fine elaborate drawing in which is shown a raven with a black body but a white head, emphasizing this idea. It is the mystical death of the body. This can again be interpreted in the light of the quotation on a former page. That is to say, that the ancients considered two deaths to be possible. The one is the natural death which occurs to all men at the close of their particular span of life. This is involuntary and inevitable. But there is another death which the sages and saints cultivate, inasmuch as it culminates in life and in fullness of spiritual perception. This is the death induced through intense meditation and contemplation, when consciousness, indrawn into itself, and dissevered from its bodily senses and functions, dies consciously and deliberately to this earthly life to function in a higher and nobler sphere.

To whiten the black is part and parcel of the same type of operation. Likewise, to vivify the white, self-immersion, or the deepest state of introversion, leads to a stimulation of the depths of the Unconscious, and an upwelling or vivification of the libido, or vital spirit. Once the process of dissolution and separation is begun, the entire nature commences to undergo a transformation and equilibriation.

Yet as averred by Eudoxus, it is in the first operation that the true and preliminary dissolution, without which nothing is of value, is begun. The dragon is the libido or vital spirit, undomesticated and untrained, as we have previously determined when examining *The Golden Treatise* of Hermes. Its blackness represents the degree in which it has become involved in matter and thus obscured ; it symbolizes the evil in which it has become immersed by reason of its subordination to the tyrannical self-willed spirit, or consciousness. The blackness again signifies the preponderance of anxiety and fear generated by consciousness, weighing it down, impeding its free circulation in the blood and bodily system, and knotting it, so to speak, in the Unconscious levels from which it is unable to escape or by which it is constantly dominated. To destroy this anxiety and to release the libido—more or less synonymous or simultaneous operations—by means of the magnetic trance is the first work. "The fire of the natural life entering into and fermenting the natural fire—the same life in another, opens the last, and develops and excites and sets free the celestial Life and Light—that is one main principle. . . ."

The result of such a state is, naturally, that upon which the whole hermetic work can proceed. Released from restriction within the body by the impact of extraneous magnetism which is the external fire, the inward fire or vitality can form a new life within. Left to itself in its freed state, the Light will circulate and form spontaneously its own new centre and vehicle. The Western alchemical conception is practically identical with that of the East. In the Chinese text, so ably translated by R. Wilhelm, there are a couple of sentences which are particularly apposite in this connection.

> The Heavenly Heart is like the dwelling-place, the Light is the master.
> Therefore when the Light circulates the powers of the whole body arrange themselves before its throne, just as when a holy king has taken possession of the capital and has laid down the fundamental rules of order, all the states approach with tribute ; or, just as when the master is quiet and calm, men-servants and maids obey his orders of their own accord, and each does his work.
> Therefore you only have to make the Light circulate : that is the deepest and most wonderful secret. The Light is easy to move, but difficult to fix. If it is allowed to go long enough in a circle, then it crystallizes itself : that is the natural spirit-body.

This is the astral Body of Light, white and resplendent, the glowing Stone of the Wise, whose purified and glorified emanations glow as the aura, some glittering and flaming jewel of incomparable scintillation, invaluable, ineffable.

One very fine occult scholar, John M. Pryse, describes the aura in his work *The Apocalypse Unsealed*. Speaking of the *kundalini*, which is the hermetic secret fire, he writes that it is this force

> which, in the telestic work, or cycle of initiation, weaves from the primal substance of the auric ovum, upon the ideal form of archetype it contains, and conforming thereto, the immortal Augoeîdes, or solar body (soma heliakon), so called because in its visible appearance it is self-luminous like the sun, and has a golden radiance. Its aureola displays a filmy opalescence. This solar body is of atomic, non-molecular substance.
>
> The psychic, or luna, body, through which the Nous acts in the psychic world, is molecular in structure, but of far finer substance than the elements composing the gross physical form, to whose organism it closely corresponds, having organs of sight, hearing, and the rest. In appearance it has a silvery lustre, tinged with delicate violet ; and its aura is of palest blue, with an interchanging play of all the prismatic colours, rendering it iridescent.

In the Pelican-phoenix references we have further rebirth symbols. Animals and birds always represent in dream symbolism—and such symbolism is the language both of the Unconscious and alchemical writing—libido substitutes. The type of the animal defines the degree of domesticity and civilization, so to speak, attained by the libido. Released from its restriction and the prison in which it has for so long been confined, the libido acts upon the entire nature through the blood, glands, and consciousness itself, to form a resplendent interior ideal form. But even this latter requires to be dissolved and fermented by its own analytical life—even as the Phoenix tears open its own breast in order to feed its young with its own life-blood. The vitality of the Stone destroys its own basis in order to renew itself. The new solar form is derived from and based upon the former crystallized mental sheath, as, of course, it must be. Compare with Osiris, who sings : "This is my body, which I destroy in order that it may be renewed."

Here the alchemical theory would seem not only to recognize but to develop the psychological theory so recently enunciated by Jung. The solution of the problem relating to the restoration of consciousness to its own divine integrity lies not exclusively in a conversion into its opposite, though this of course is necessary. Actually such a process is imperative, for without this conversion consciousness would be cut off from its archetypal roots and would tremble in mid-air without adequate support. But the true solution lies in the retention of the former values of consciousness plus a recognition of their dynamic opposites in the personal unconsciousness.

So that, in speaking of this particular stage represented as the Pelican—a definite stage of progress—alchemy announces that this libido-symbol too is to be destroyed, or overcome. Its point of view is partitive—even as is that of consciousness whose nature is to be transcended. We have here, it seems to me, a description of the transcendent function described by that master of European analytical psychology. For the text says that the Stone as it exists at this juncture—that is, full awareness of the opposite of consciousness—is to be dissolved. That is, the libido, or the spiritual energy, retreating before the apparently insoluble conflict—the play between the conscious and the unconscious—regresses and goes back even farther than the memories of early infancy. It sinks back into the depths or deposits of racial or ancestral life, and the mythological images resident in these profound levels of the unconscious awaken.

Thus "begins the separation of the elements in a philosophical manner". The task confronting the patient or the student is to differentiate the elements of his own personal unconscious from the primordial archetypes or dominants of the collective unconscious, to enable the psychical energy to well up, activating and vitalizing the faculties and powers of consciousness itself. This separation of the personal from the impersonal, and this differentiation of the ego and the non-ego, overcomes the intolerable pull of the opposites within the sphere of the patient, making possible a reconciliation which produces a therapeutic and integrating effect upon his consciousness.

The Pelican, it may be remarked in conclusion of this

symbolism, possesses under its bill a great pouch in which it can preserve food, principally fish. If it wishes to regurgitate the food out of its crop to feed its young, it must rest its bill against its breast. It is conceivable that from this appearance there developed the legend that it tore open its breast in order to feed its young with its own life-blood. From early times the Pelican was therefore used as a symbol of Christ, who shed his blood to redeem mankind—markedly a collective symbol. The alchemists represented the Philosopher's Stone, the red tincture, as a Pelican or the more fabulous Phoenix. For by its projection on the baser metals of its own personality it sacrificed itself and, as it were, gave its blood to tinct them. The libido thus no longer activates exclusively the primordial depths, but the ego, the child, can make use of it too.

Certain of the latter alchemists have employed the Christ symbolism to represent the Stone. Bringing Christ to birth within the soul of man is a fitting symbolism for such an operation.

In the second key is a continuation of the Pelican theme. The newly formed Stone must be dissolved. The purification has not proceeded sufficiently far to render it permanent. The work cannot be accomplished by one operation. The trance state must be continued again and again, and persisted in until consciousness finally eclipses itself, when it proceeds spontaneously to evolve in an entirely new direction. Again the separation of the pure from the impure must be achieved. The spirit, vitality, must be separated from every level and type of consciousness, its soul and vehicle. This accomplished, then the very elements which constitute the residue can be changed and sublimated—or redirected into new and worthier channels.

2. The central secret of the entire work is now approached. When employing the psychological method, we associated the emotions and feelings with the philosophical Fire. When using the magnetic interpretation, this correspondence did not seem very much to help us. We must look elsewhere for a further and more complete explanation. There is the interpretation that the Fire is the penetrating power of the intellect, and this sometimes is the

sense in which the author of *The Suggestive Inquiry into the Hermetic Mystery* interprets the mystery of the secret fire. Various writers at various times have identified it with a spiritual principle permeating and pervading the universe. Others identify it with the fiery power of will. Possibly from all these hints we can proceed a step farther, and by amalgamation and synthesis produce a workable hypothesis.

"Behind will stands desire." So runs an alchemical aphorism. This can be assumed to imply that desire directs will, and gives to it an object to achieve. Or else it may imply that the basis or background of the Will is desire or emotion, and that the former has grown out of the latter, as an evolution or sublimation, even as consciousness depends upon the Unconscious. The motive power of the instinctual life is the libido, desire, the vital spirit, while the motive power of the intellectual life is the Will. In its developments and peregrinations, in its eclipse by the magnetic trance state, the will loses its former sense of direction. But having almost reached the verge of annihilation, so to speak, reaching the nadir of its life, it restores itself by an effort which is mighty beyond words. One step towards this divine restoration is the fierceness of its fire and heat, as though desperation towards life urged forth every ounce of inherent vitality. At this stage, when it associates itself with and is given life by desire, the emotional nature, it is often called the Vitriol of Venus or the Green Lion, both implying the volitional power of penetration, fiery and crude, of immature but evolving spiritual energy.

> But it's because of the transcendent force
> It hath ; and for the rawness of its source,
> Of which the like is nowhere to be seene,
> That yt of us is named the Lyon Greene.

So wrote the Vicar of Malden some centuries ago.
Mrs. Atwood observes that :

> The cause of the dissolution appears to proceed from the action of the vital heat stirred up artificially in the blood, and which, being so continuously triturated,

ignites and opens for itself a passage, endeavouring forthwith to absorb the circulating light by the efflux of its own abundant chloric spirit being transfixed.

In reality it is more than a suggestion that we find here—obscure though the passage may be. In order to explain the implication of this passage, and the whole of the Atwood mesmeric hypothesis, it is necessary that we resort to various references in comparative religion, or at least to their practical aspects as may be perceived in such mystical arts as Yoga, Tantra, and meditation. From a study of Tibetan Yogic practices we know that the development of the so-called external psychic heat—which permits the anchorite to live on mountain heights several thousand feet above sea level clad only in a single cotton garment—is achieved by various forms of breathing. Let me quote a short passage from Dr. Evans Wentz's recent work *Tibetan Yoga and Secret Doctrines*, which deals precisely with this subject. He says :

> The first of these (the six doctrines) is known to the Tibetans as *Tummo*, signifying a peculiar bodily heat, or warmth, of psycho-physical character, generated by *yogic* means. According to the secret lore, the word *Tummo* refers to a method of extracting *prana* from the inexhaustible *pranic* reservoir in Nature, and storing it in the human-body battery and then employing it to transmute the generative fluid into a subtle fiery energy whereby a psycho-physical heat is produced internally and made to circulate through the nerve-channels of the psychic nervous system. . . . According to our text, in practising the art of *Tummo* the *yogin* must employ very elaborate visualizations, meditations, postures, breathings, directing of thought, training of the psychic-nerve system, and physical exercises.

But as in Hatha Yoga and Tantra, great stress is laid upon the breathings themselves as the most important factor involved. The directions given in the Eastern texts as to the length of breathing, retention, and exhalation are very precise and elaborate. It is significant enough that any ordinary person can produce quite a copious perspiration within a few minutes by means of regulated deep breathing and retentions.

The Yoga theory, which is very similar, and is in fact that from which the Tibetan one has been borrowed, stipulates that in the air, quite apart from the combustible oxygen, is something which they call *Prana*, or life. But in order to illustrate the relationship of life and breath within the concept of the dynamic spiritual principle permeating all things, it is worth recapitulating the Hindu idea. Life, or *prana*, they say, is a universally pervasive principle. It is the vital ocean in which the earth itself floats ; it permeates the entire globe and every being and object on it. It works unceasingly on and around us, pulsating against and through us for ever. In life we merely use a very specialized instrument, more so than any other, for dealing with both *Prana* and *Jiva*. Strictly speaking, *Prana* is breath. As breath is necessary for continuance of life in the human machine, the Hindu philosophy considers that that is the best word. *Jiva*, on the other hand, means "life", and also is applied to the living soul, for the life in general is derived from the supreme universal spirit itself. *Jiva* is therefore capable of general application as referring to the infinite and ubiquitous spirit ; whilst *prana* is more particular as implying that specialized flow of life which permeates the human frame.

Parts of the mystical training of Yoga demand a prolonged charging of the entire system with an enormous amount of *Prana*, thus rendering the body rather like a powerful storage battery. Since, according to the theory delineated above, there is some connection between air and spirit on the one hand, and between the rate of inspiration and the motion of the mind on the other hand, illumination and spiritual attainment may be achieved by this technical method. So also is the psychic heat attained by the Tibetan hermit.

From the practical point of view the Yoga theory demands a retirement from the world, or that a great deal of time and attention be devoted to these practices. Hours each day must be spent in mastering difficult postures, and in acquiring skill in pranayama and meditation. According to the record of one practitioner that some years ago was shown to me, eight hours a day was devoted to pranayama before finally a minor illumination flooded the mind. Clearly such a course is impossible for the average man of the West, no matter how great his sympathy for the Eastern ideal. He has at least two thousand years of incessant activity, commercial bustle, and materialistic preoccupation behind him. It would be a violation of his nature and his racial heredity to refute his ancestry and adopt the Eastern hermit life.

Hence it is by some contended that the alchemistic and mesmeric theory is almost an ideal adaptation principally for such an individual. It is a European version of the Eastern Yoga technique, developed essentially for the evolving Western man. Since one phase of Yoga has as its primary object the deliberate and willed absorption of enormous quantities of spiritual energy, the Western methods adopt the same theory in its broad outlines. But its practice proceeds along entirely different lines. Magnetism, or prana, is imparted from operator to subject by the usual magnetic practical methods and then thrown back again by the subject to the former operator. In so doing it undergoes a fermentation and acceleration. As the presence of power increases and induces power, so the continual trituration and friction of the vital spirit causes an increase both of the energy and its potency. Its intensity is augmented to a degree which is inconceivable. Its voltage, so to speak, is increased, the psychic state opened thereby transcending the mere impassivity of the ordinary mesmeric trance—developing slowly but gradually a charge or flow of libido which becomes so powerful in its intensity and quality as well to be named the Secret Fire of the Wise.

Having thus dilated and enlarged upon the fundamental bases of the Atwood hypothesis and compared it briefly with the Yoga practice of pranayama, it may be worth while to give Mrs. Atwood's own theory in her own words. First of all she castigates the modern (about 1850) practice of the Mesmeric art in these terms.

If, then, we go out at once to throw our common life to common lives (that is, impart our own unpurified and undeveloped *prana* to equally unpurified subjects), what wonder we have only common results? That much depends upon the quality of the life imparted, general

I

observation teaches ; and with what sure corresponding consequences the moral leaven is attended may be understood, in a degree, by the recipient in the mesmeric trance. But the spontaneous fermentation which the Vital Spirit undergoes, and the change that is thereby effected in the Passive Subject, is not taken advantage of in modern practice or pushed to the uttermost ; much less is understood that exact art of grafting and transplanting which the ancients practised, and by means of which a growth and sublimation of the Spirit was effected.

And again, in describing the technical method whereby the grafting of the Vital Spirit proceeds, she declares :

As this life, being fermented by this life, its similar, leads into the common trance, or is entranced, so that consequent life, being fermented by its similar, leads into that third life which moves in and with the Creative Essence, so that the mind becomes in that case related to the Universal Vitalizing Power, and so can act Its will. . . . The fire of the natural life entering into and fermenting the natural fire—the same life in another, opens the last and develops and excites and sets free the celestial life and Light—that is one main principle. . . . When one life being fermented throws its life to another equally fermented, a greater perfection is produced in the patient than was before in the agent who imparts it. That is the law of progression of the vital force—*sic itur ad astra.*

It is in this last couple of sentences where the really significant secret is contained. It is in the transference of spiritual vitality, consciously and deliberately, from operator to subject, and back again, and retransferring the dynamic charge to subject, continuing the process again and again, which develops the latent fire and awakens the life of the concealed and latent spirit. There are several methods already known to us for the fermentation or augmentation of the individual spiritual power interiorly. Several of these I have summarized and described in my former work *The Middle Pillar.* Simplest among such methods is the art of rhythmic breathing. The ordinary Yoga theory postulates that the most familiar mechanism for dealing with and thus controlling and augmenting *prana* is the machinery of the lungs. By deliberately establishing a slow, measured rhythm of exhalation and inhalation of the breath, whilst formulating in the mind the idea of absorbing vitality from the universe about one, the body and mind become very considerably charged with vitality. The method is exceedingly simple, requiring only a little patience and practice to become quite adept with it, and to benefit in no inconsiderable way by the increase of vitality and power which it imparts.

A second method, rather more complex than the above, is that known as the Middle Pillar technique, of which a brief description appears in *The Art of True Healing*. Its procedure is fundamentally simple, providing for the imaginative formulation of various centres of Light placed on a shaft penetrating the body from the crown of the head to the soles of the feet. Names are imagined to vibrate therein, and the combination of thought, sound, and colour awakens these centres to an equilibriated activity within. Such an activity throws into the psycho-physical system vast quantities of high-powered spiritual energy. This power, too, can be transmitted from one person to another with the greatest of ease, and that by a simple manual contact. It is my contention that anyone, sceptic or otherwise, by following the simple directions so far as the practical instructions are concerned, can prove for himself the validity of the magnetic hypothesis. Using this method for working up steam, as it were, as a preliminary to the practical application of the more complex and advanced Atwood technique, considerable results should be obtained. In this connection it is worth stressing 'my belief that on the whole magnetic "passes" do not conduce to a satisfactory transmission of power. There is considerable wastage of energy in so far as the method is not sufficiently direct. The Eeman method as described in *Self and Superman* should be studied as being most useful. The technique described by de Puységur is extremely efficient, and is really a vast improvement on the passes. That is to say, the operator places one hand over the solar plexus or spleen of the patient and the other on the latter's head. Linked up in this way, he imagines himself to be a storage battery absorbing power from the universe and "pumping" it into his patient. Within a very few minutes both he and the patient obtain the marked sensation of such transmission. Accompanying the Middle Pillar technique by rhythmic breathing enables the operator to absorb enormous quantities of vitality from the atmosphere and the universe about him, thus rendering fatigue an extreme improbability. So long as the operator definitely realizes, with humility and a lack of egotism, that he is but a channel through which the cosmic forces may flow, his ability to transmit energy is never impeded. If we consider the realm of therapy, it is only when successful cures imbue him with a sense of self-importance that trouble begins. He comes to consider himself as a powerful healer, stressing his own personal abilities and forgetting that the spiritual power is not his own. Thus the channels become blocked, and there is a temporary cessation in the flow of the spirit through him.

With the channels wide open, vitality flows without impediment through the personality, and the application of the techniques of rhythmic breathing and the Middle Pillar will enable both operator and subject to fulfil easily the requirements of the Atwood hypothesis. Vitality as ordinarily experienced is of little value. But the power that invades the personality during the Middle Pillar practice is of such a nature as will, when transmitted by the hands, ferment the being of the subject. If, after some time, the subject changes his rôle and becomes the operator and throws back the vitality to the former operator, who now becomes the subject, a considerable psychic change develops.

The common assumption that mesmeric methods are dangerous does not require much consideration. All forms of therapy in one sense or another are dangerous. The whole of life is dangerous. The mere attempt to cross a modern street is an undertaking which is fraught with the utmost danger when one considers the extreme probability that the turbulent surge of traffic may find yet another victim. All the hypnotic authorities refute the charge that the practice of hypnotism has a deleterious effect upon the patient. Many of them cite subjects who have been hypnotized hundreds of times without the least injurious result. On the other hand, it is easy to see that in the hands of an unscrupulous and dishonest operator serious harm may be effected. Nevertheless, this latter argument is true also of medical and psychological practice. One has to be certain of the integrity and trustworthiness of one's physician or psychologist before submitting to treatment.

A second objection is likewise without foundation. It asserts that the practice of mesmerism interferes with the free function of the will, which faculty is precisely that which should operate in the study of occultism. Hypnotism has been defined as an artificial method of obtaining a concentrated or abstracted state. It thus resembles meditation or concentration, when consciousness or the attention has been withdrawn from the outside world and is focused upon one solitary idea. The difference is that in the former case the meditator is assisted by a second person, whilst in the other the state is self-induced. Thus, from one point of view, it is said that the latter is infinitely superior in that one is not dependent upon any other person, being self-reliant and capable of controlling both the mind and the psychic faculties. One advocate of this point of view, Dr. Evans Wentz, writing in his most recent book, asserts that European critics of Yoga have thought that such practices induce a sort of self-hypnotism. If, in some degree, the criticism be well founded, we must, nevertheless, take into account the fact that hypnotization by one's own efforts has a far different result, in so far as experimental knowledge is concerned, than hypnotization by another person. In self-hypnotization the *yogin* is wholly the master of himself, whereas in hypnotic trance induced in one person by another the hypnotized subject loses mastery of himself and is more or less enslaved to the will of the hypnotizer, and upon being released from hypnosis has little or no conscious memory of the nature of the hypnotic state or the character of the mind's reactions to the external stimuli inducing that state.

It is only necessary to observe that this phenomenon of amnesia can be remedied quite easily with repeated hypnosis and by training. In fact, to adopt what is in my opinion a balanced and sane attitude one might state that an ideal form of training would be the conjoining of the analytical procedure of psychology, the induction of the mesmeric or somnambulistic state, and the practice of one of the occult meditation techniques. By these three methods any deficiency inherent in any particular technique could be remedied, and consciousness itself could be considerably enhanced.

So far as concerns the accusation that Yoga or meditation practices induce self-hypnotism, since that is assumed in a derogatory manner, much depends on the definition of hypnosis. On this subject there exists so much confusion, fear, and wrong thinking, due probably to the past abuses of theatrical performers besides the romantic speculations of some too-imaginative novelists, that it is necessary to resort to a definition expressed on a former page. That is to say, in a few words, that the state induced by hypnosis is comparable in every respect to a condition of extreme introspection. The major difference is that the subject is assisted in the production of this one-pointed condition by a second person guiding his consciousness along a predetermined track. Being in a highly concentrated mood, consciousness is far more accessible to (a) upwellings of formerly unconscious material and to (b) the implanting of suggestions for the furtherance of certain ends and for the evocation of corresponding faculties within. It all depends on how this condition is used as to whether good, that is desirable, results shall follow, or whether failure be one's reward.

The ideal of being "wholly the master of himself" in the case of the *yogin* is, from one point of view and from a legitimate and valid angle of argument, an instance of excessive individualism. In the East the idea of co-operation between groups of people has never risen to the practical heights that the West, regardless of other of its defects, has achieved. It is far more common for Europeans to work one with another than is the case in the East. There it may be a commonly observed phenomenon for disciples to flock to gurus, but in the majority of instances it is hardly an organized affair. Consequently, the Eastern system is prone to elevate its own weakness, making a sublime virtue of what in reality is a psychological and neurotic defect. It is the old story of the fox who lost his tail. In the West, co-operation as an ideal has gradually developed and slowly has been reaching its fruition. Therefore, even in spiritual and psychological things, we here see no harm in receiving assistance and support from some other person. We consider it the most natural thing to do so. And, so it is argued, there can thus be no harm in the use of mesmerism or hypnosis as a means of obtaining proficiency in the meditative art *provided* in addition the subject is aware of two things. One, the integrity of his guide or teacher, so that he experiences no hesitancy or apprehension in submitting to the induction of hypnosis. And, two, that he realizes that in the last resort he must stand upon his own feet, and that to rely exclusively upon the operator is a confession of extreme weakness which can be dangerous to his spiritual welfare.

This, at any rate, seems to be the import of the Atwood technique—a method whereby the co-operation of two interested individuals is employed towards a certain end, and that a spiritual one. With the proposed disintegration of the astro-mental sheath by a magnetic surplus, so to say, the theory holds that it is possible for the locked-up libido to be released and ascend more readily to the higher levels of consciousness, there being available for general and immediate use. The two operations are synonymous and occur simultaneously. The deliberate breaking-down of the crystallized elements of the personal sphere spontaneously releases the power latent within them. This release is tantamount to a sublimation. That is to say it is a transfer of energy from a lower form of activity or level of consciousness to a higher. And, as our text indicates, until this locked-up energy is released no further steps are possible.

Indeed, this position is analogous to the Yoga system. No knowledge, true non-illusory knowledge, of the universe and of life is really possible without first having experienced some degree of Samadhi, the mystical experience. This attainment is engineered by several means, chief amongst which being the technique of arousing the coiled-up, latent power called Kundalini, stored at the base of the spine. Once aroused, this power must be guided up the Sushumna in the spine to the brain. This ascent of vital energy to the psycho-mental chakra in the brain, or rather above the crown of the head, induces a condition of consciousness which is characterized by the immediate acquisition of intuitive knowledge and by the experiencing of an ineffable bliss which is unlike any other experience in life. At the same time the realization of complete and absolute freedom is obtained, as though every bond which tied one to the world and linked the world to one's own self were severed. In a word, the mechanisms of introjection and projection of psychic qualities are realized in full consciousness, and overcome. Having thus experienced Samadhi, the Yogi, being free for the first time, detached, and no longer enslaved either by extraneous or subjective circumstances, can envisage life as it really is. As a consequence he can contemplate what further steps should be taken for his own evolution. And he will also see in a way that few other beings can see how he may help and not hinder his fellow man.

The second Key of Eudoxus informs us that the unfolding of the nature of consciousness cannot be undertaken without the preliminary dissolution of conscious restriction and inhibitions. The entire mental sheath must be broken down in order that its psychic constituents may be rearranged in a modified and better form. Following upon this, the sublimation of libido can be accomplished. This condition of sublimation achieved, then the conversion of the elements is possible—that is, reconstructing the Robe of Glory, the inner Body of Light—as well as the extraction and full realization in consciousness of the three Principles. These three Principles have been likened to Selflessness, with its opposite of Self for Mercury; Change, with its opposite of Stability for Sulphur ; and Sorrow, with its implicit of Bliss for Salt. That is to say, these operations must permit the latent qualities and divine powers dormant in the various levels of the psyche, unknown and unsuspected by the ego, to expand and attain their maximum expression and development.

4. The Sun and Moon are astrological symbols for male and female, positive and negative, the psychological equivalents of Consciousness and the *Anima* (or *Animus*) principle. The union of these two dissevered constituents of the personality creates integrity and unity of being. And it is only the *whole* man, the equilibriated and balanced individual, who can truly initiate. The distillation is the spiritual energy

which would circulate in such a person. It is this distillation which requires to be manumitted to the prepared subject. There it can ferment, and after repeated transferences arouse that interior secret fire of the spirit within the blood which will dissolve the dull and unpurified stone. The great Sea of the Wise is, as we previously determined, the Collective Unconsciousness, or the higher divine Astral plane, the ubiquitous all-pervasive storehouse of magnetism, vitality, feeling, and memory.

5. Dissolved in this way, into what, for lack of other and better words, may be termed a homogeneous magnetic fluid, the Stone may well be called the Vine of the Wise. As these hermetic processes go forward, and the fluidic substance matures and develops in the right direction, it is known as the philosophical Wine. The Wine is extracted from the Vine—that is, the dissolved constituents of the entire personality which, because of this dissolution, evinces a possibility of further and new growth. The Wine represents the same substance symbolized by the Vine, but on a higher plane. Because of the attention we have given to it, and the processes to which we have subjected it, the wine we extract and develop from the grape vine is a higher development of the source from which it came. In that sense it is an evolution. We could likewise suggest that the Unconscious is the Vine, and the libido, which issues from the hidden depths of the psyche, answers to the Wine of which Eudoxus so enigmatically speaks. So far as this alchemical Wine is concerned, as it continues to be subjected to the coction and influence of the fire, further development increases its virulence, so to speak, at which junction it is denominated as a most sharp Vinegar. It is an acid fluid continuing the process of disintegration yet further and in a more subtle way invading the entire mental and psychic sphere, as a preliminary to the reconstruction of the sphere of sensation on a better and diviner plan.

Some mention must be made of the consequent alteration in the blood-stream caused by glandular secretions stimulated and equilibriated by changes in both feeling and consciousness induced by the Great Work. It is an empirical fact that mental and emotional changes are capable of inducing changes in the blood-stream and in the tissue structure of the physical body. We are all familiar with instances of sudden and unexpected bad news at meal-times which has induced vomiting. The study of neurosis has also provided us with innumerable examples of nervous and physical disturbances induced by adverse psychic activity. It is a psychological fact that neurasthenia, constipation, indigestion, arthritis, pruritis, and many other ailments are direct results of psychological causes. Sometimes to deal with the psychogenic factors eliminates or relieves physical symptoms. At others, direct physical therapy of different kinds is required to relieve mental symptoms of distress. In other words, mind and body may not be considered as two separate entities. The more accurate viewpoint might be that they are two poles of a single entity, two different functions adopted by that entity for the purpose of obtaining experience and dealing with external life. They constitute, with the additional postulate of occult philosophy of an astro-mental body, a direct continuum. Changes therefore occurring anywhere along that continuum, affecting any link, must produce inevitably a result or change in some other part of the chain. Though I am not aware of any definite experiments, it ought to be possible to show that the blood-specimens of hypnotic-trance subjects exhibit alterations and a slightly different chemical composition from those of ordinary persons. Hence in dealing with such powerful media as meditation, magnetism, and the reverse transmission of vitality, we are fairly certain to find that physical effects should ensue. Transmutation thus becomes an actual physiological and experimental fact, the entire physical frame becoming more sensitive, purified, and responsive to the delicate impulses transmitted to and from the consciousness dwelling within.

Third Key. As we proceed in the examination of these Keys, the material becomes more and more obscure. The only saving grace is that we are counselled to continue as we have begun. Because of this advice, and because I have been more prolix in the commentary to the two previous keys, I do not propose to examine the entirety of this third Key or those remaining. After noting certain points in the first half of this key, I see no further necessity to continue.

The student, in the light of the preceding chapters, can examine the text as he wishes.

2. The principal operation to be undertaken according to the description of this Key is the extraction of the three principles of Salt, Sulphur, and Mercury from the comparatively homogeneous base called the Water of the Wise, or our Mercury. This is accomplished, as Eudoxus informs us, by a "perfect dissolution and glorification of the body whence it had its nativity". It is also furthered or engineered by means of the Spirit, or Sulphur—the end being the union of the soul with the body. Elsewhere this process is termed "fixing the volatile". The soul would correspond to the airy volatile nature of consciousness, Mercury, and it requires to be fixed or coagulated in a more or less solid foundation of the Salt, the body. And the text further clarifies the issue in the next verse : "This is the Intention, and the essential point of the operations of this Key, which terminate at the generation of a new substance infinitely nobler than the first."

4. Slowly the issue becomes clearer, carrying on the exegesis from the end of the second Key. Eudoxus speaks of the homogeneous substance, the philosophical Water, concealing the Three principles which are comparable to the spirit, soul, and (subtle) body. Here Eudoxus emphasizes a fact which I stated above. For these three principles, like every other thing in nature, are not pure in their natural state, and to be purified need to be banished and separated prior to re-amalgamation. Hence the process begun originally requires to be continued so that a distillation is made of the homogeneous and amorphous astral base. A separation then occurs. A cleavage takes place, dividing the natural unity of Mercury and Sulphur, soul and spirit, from their vehicle, the Salt. This earth, or Salt, remains fixed within the physical body "like a dead, black, and dreggy earth". Its life departed, the subtle sheath turns to putrefaction and decay.

5. But even this dreg is of untold value. Nothing in the alchemical art is discarded, for "Nature teaches us" so assert the *Chaldaean Oracles*, "and the Oracles also affirm that even the evil germs of matter may alike be made useful and good". In her *Memorabilia* Mrs. Atwood remarks that "the principle of body is preserved in what they call the ashes, or

Caput Mortum, and that, one principle being saved, the whole life is restored from it ; Khunrath calls it 'our pigmy', also the 'diadem of the body'. . . ."

6. Latent within the blackness of the ashes is life—inter-atomic life, which by no means can be snuffed out, and which sooner or later asserts itself, communicating movement and life to the mass.   There is a Qabalistic aphorism which has it that "*Keser*" (spirit or whiteness) "is in *Malkus*" (matter or blackness) "and *Malkus* is in *Keser*, but after another manner". And again, it is said that within the material extreme of life, when it is purified, the Seed of the Spirit is at last found. Ultimately, there can be no distinction made between spirit and matter. The latter is a crystallization of the former, and spirit is a rarefied and sublimed form of matter. Matter is composed of molecules, these of atoms. By analysis the atoms are seen to be composed of still smaller particles, protons and electrons. These are considered to be positive and negative charges of electricity, whilst the latter, as energy, is a light radiation, the manifestation of the spirit in action. It is by the persistent subjection of the dregs to the fire of the Wise that the innate and implicit spiritual life and energy is stirred to renewed and desperate activity. The blackness is cast off, and the Salt is washed and purified. By these purgative means it is fixed, becoming the blood or the life of the Stone, the immortal substantive and energetic basis of the regenerated consciousness.

7. Fire and Water, being opposite, are yet mutually attractive. It is the age-old philosophy which is here ex-pounded. Spirit is the antithesis of Matter. Yet the attrac-tion of the one for the other is so great that, like man and woman, male and female everywhere, without the other each is lost and incomplete. The union therefore of spirit and soul is enjoined on us with great and emphasized ear-nestness. The one is the universal, all-pervasive life-force, whilst the other is an individualized particular unit of that energy, made self-conscious through experience and im-mersion in matter. This union, apparently, can only take place through a third thing. They themselves are so extreme that it would seem impossible for them ever to be conjoined. Just as, with regard to an attitude towards life, it is com-paratively easy to choose some one extreme viewpoint and

follow that to the end. But it is infinitely more difficult to envisage the two opposites in consciousness and attempt their union. Such an attempt is always foredoomed to failure. But one can succeed by formulating an entirely new point of view which does not consist exclusively of either of the two opposites. Or, to state it more properly, the ego reconciles them because it has risen above them. More technically, the spirit itself, or the libido, by regression to the Collective Unconscious, reconciles and unites them.

Thus it is that the alchemical tradition asserts that the union of the individual soul with the universal spirit can only ensue through the mediation of a third thing, the Earth, or the subtle Body of Light. It is this which is the medium and link between mind and matter.

8. To repeat and to emphasize is oftimes to clarify. The author of this cryptic text now adds that fire and water, though of different genders or polarities, are fundamentally and essentially of the same nature. These are separated from their material basis by the mechanical and continued application of fire. Having achieved a separation, the material basis, the Salt, is to be moistened occasionally by its water. That is, Mercury, actuated by Sulphur, which gives it volition, is to moisten or impregnate or indwell its former vehicle now *in extremis*.

What formerly took place in archaic prehistoric epochs as an involuntary act of nature, now occurs with the full consciousness of the spirit. There is a descent of the spirit into matter, even as the gods of the solar myths descended into the underworld—repeating the original operations or phases occurring in cosmic evolution. This descent moistens Earth with the Water, and also fixes the Spirit. The occurrence is dual in nature. The union of Salt and Sulphur, the two opposites, brings to birth once more the individual consciousness, formerly eclipsed by the magnetic trance and the vital transfer. It may at first be thought that the joining of spirit and matter in this manner after their previous separation produces the identical unity which prevailed before. In point of fact this is not so, and the alchemists are adamant in their insistence upon the difference. Just as, in a magical ceremony, the invocation of an element into a clearer space after its prior banishing is not the same element as obtained before, but a purer quintessence of it, so by the spagyric art the unity of Salt, Sulphur, and Mercury appears "under a more noble and more perfect form that it was before".

Another commentator chose to interpret this union as between *Ruach*, the mind or ego, and *Neschamah*, the Higher Soul or Fiery Mind, understanding. After this mystical union the elevated *Ruach* returns as master to its proper union with *Nephesch*, the animal soul, whose nature is thus fulfilled.

9. The Stone we have already determined to be a term covering several concepts. At times it is a multiple concept including the three alchemical principles together. At other times, like the word Mercury, it refers to the Quintessence, the crown and synthesis of the elements. On still other occasions it has application alone to the substantive principle of Salt, which is referred on the Qabalistic Tree to the Sephirah *Hod*, Splendour, to the element of Water, to the astrological planet Mercury, both these latter attributions representing energy and plasticity and fluidity of substance, the substance of the so-called astral sheath or Body of Light.

This paragraph teaches that from the Stone, the generic term for the homogeneous compound, issues Water. This divine Water can only be realized by our fiery dissolution. Here it becomes necessary to extend the significations of our elemental attributions. These symbols are infinitely elastic. In certain forms of occult symbolism, to the Sephirah *Hod* is attributed the symbol of the cup. This Cup has a special shape to express in symbolic form fundamental ideas. The base of the Cup is triangular, or rather pyramidal. Upon this rests a circle, or sphere, whilst above this is a crescent, the actual bowl of the Cup. This can be made to yield several significant meanings. The base, being triangular, is the type and symbol of fire. Being pyramidal, it represents every aspect of fire—astral, solar, and terrestrial fire. The circular symbol, by employing the symbology of the Hindu tattwa system, refers to the element of Air. Above the circle is the crescent, which by the same system of symbolism is attributed to the element of Water. But see the section on symbols in Volume One of *The Golden Dawn*.

Now, in their broadest significations, these three elements refer to the three fundamental divisions or aspects of man's psyche. The triangle of fire is attributed to the instinctive and emotional principle. Air, as we have previously determined, is the elemental characteristic of the mind ; thus the circle represents consciousness. The spiritual part of man, his aspirations and higher yearnings, his intuition and imagination, is represented by the crescent. Thus Air, consciousness, is the reconciler between the opposites. Man, symbolized by this formal symbol, is thus represented as a complete psychic entity open always, if he will, to the influx of *Keser*, the universal spirit of life.

Fig. 3.—CUP SYMBOLISM

The employment of Water at this particular stage in our alchemical text implies the gradual coming into operation of a spiritual principle. By the dissolution of the bonds that cramp and bind consciousness, chains that hold it in thralldom to purely illusory concepts in conflict with reality, the inner spiritual life is released. This spiritual life is that which is represented by Water.

10. Various properties and names are assigned to this fluid—depending upon certain stages reached in the working. But I gather that as the work is begun, through increasing the potency of the inward fire by a constant trituration and transfer, so it is continued. It is this which accomplishes the distillation.

That this Water has a lofty significance can hardly

be doubted when one remembers the references in both sections of Scripture. Remember the passages in Revelations : "And he showed me a pure river of water of life, clear as crystal, proceeding out of the throne of God and of the Lamb." And again : "I am Alpha and Omega, the beginning and the end. I will give unto him that is athirst of the fountain of the water of life freely."

12. Reiteration continues to emphasize that dissolution again is the preliminary operation. The subtle body, now separated from its informing principle, must be dissolved into its own homogeneous astral base, the Salt. It is this further process of dissolution which actually releases the full fiery blast of the inner fire.

The first applications of the alchemical fire are slow and gentle. Necessarily so. Gradually its heat increases to a full and high intensity as the bodily and astral system slowly becomes accustomed to its force. And it is this which, in time, produces the blackness of putrefaction in the body, which is the signal so desired. Future success in this type of working depends entirely and exclusively on this condition having been reached.

The precept of Senior quoted in the text is an extremely interesting one, and those who have followed exegesis and have further applied their own intuitions may recognize its implication. The highest fume is the vital spirit which in its temporary eclipse is reduced to the depths. Mercury is the "divine Water" "descending from heaven", which by invading the psyche reduces or breaks down the astral form to its component principles or element. More accurately, so far as interpretation is concerned, we may assume that the psychological method is best applicable here. Mercury is the intellect pursuing the reductive method at first, and then synthesizing all things. At all events, the balm of life, which is the divine fire—as distinguished from the cruder elemental fire characterizing the lower and earlier forms of procedure —is concealed within the black ashes of the disintegrated body.

As remarked earlier, our symbolism switches over to, or is extended to include, the Supernals. The latter is a triad of divine powers commonly referred to as a unity. The trinity may be likened to the noumena or the divine roots of the elements, or the three aspects or facets of the Higher Soul, of the core of the Self, the It, and its vehicles of Wisdom, Will, and Understanding. This unit is latent and completely dormant within the blackest ashes of matter and mind until, when apparently life itself is extinct, it stirs itself spontaneously into a new and emancipated revival. So awakened into renewed existence, its action upon its concealing form is that of a purifying fire, of cleansing water, eliminating

Fig. 4.—CADUCEUS SYMBOLISM

the last remaining fragments of impurity and blackness and evil. "Your water shall be animated with this fiery essence, which works all the wonders of our art."

There is another symbolic form representing the principles inhering within the psyche which may prove a little enlightening. Its basis is the Caduceus of Mercury. The mode of interpretation employs what are called the three Mother Letters of the Hebrew Alphabet. These are Aleph, Mem, and Shin. These have elemental attributions. Since in the Qabalistic philosophy all things in the cosmos, and

K

consequently within man's psyche, have issued from the thre emajor elements, rightly they may be called Mothers. On the Caduceus, the letter Shin, **ש** three-pronged, is symbolic of the two overshadowing wings, with the central stem. In the middle is the letter Aleph, **א**, to symbolize the two heads and necks of the crossing serpents. Whilst · below is the letter Mem, **מ**, symbolizing the rest of the intertwined serpents' bodies. Thus we have the reverse of the Cup symbolism, which was a passive and receptive symbol, whereas the use of the three Mother letters is an active and masculine symbol. For above is the Fire, the letter Shin, whose numerical equivalent is a Hebrew phrase meaning the Spirit of the Gods, or the divine Spirit. It is reminiscent of that holy inspiring fire which descended upon the apostles, blessing and sanctifying them at Pentecost, endowing them with the gift of tongues. Inspiration, religious, mystical, and artistic, is the result of its descent into the barrenness of man's psyche. Consciousness, the two serpent-heads, is the letter Aleph referred to the element Air, for varying reasons which elsewhere we have discussed. Below is Mem, the passional nature of man, his animal soul, watery, turbulent, and stormy at times ; at others tending to reduce him to inertia and inactivity.

Other interpretations of this fundamental symbolism may occur to the reader. But it is hardly necessary here to enter all the intricacies of interpretation. My object was primarily to suggest various forms of exegesis, and provide the barest outline of a means of such interpretation.

Finally, and to conclude, there is one important and very difficult problem to consider. The basis of our interpretations, be they psychological, mesmeric, or magical, have all to do not with the physical substance known as gold but with the production of an illumined condition of the psyche. By comparison with the psychic state of the average individual, such illumination may well be gold as a symbol by way of comparison with the gross lead of normality. There are other interpretations, naturally, and quite possibly there is a legitimate metallurgical one. If such is the case, I do not know it. It may be left in the hands of metallurgists and chemists, for it does not concern my interests.

What is of concern, however, is the claim made by certain

students of occultism and alchemy, which is this : that
the production of spiritual changes within the psyche, and
the accomplishment of the interior transmutation, brings
to light hidden powers previously dormant and latent in
consciousness. As a bald statement this is not so improbable.
The protagonists of this theory, however, go further. They
say that these powers are such as to give their possessor the
ability, for instance, to perform a physical transmutation.
It is not impossible, they hold, to turn lead or other base
metals into gold through the mediation of the inner psychic
and spiritual faculties developed and stimulated by the
spiritual transmutation of the psyche. Whether any such
illuminated person would consider it worth while to
attempt such transmutation is quite another story, though
history affirms such attempts—moreover, successful attempts.

Arthur Edward Waite, in his work *The Secret Tradition
in Alchemy*, prefers to ignore fundamental facts in occultism
as well as the evidence of contemporary psychical research.
He uses his customary heavy artillery of criticism against
this theory where a much simpler method of consideration
would have been appropriate. He purports to despise this
theory of the psychic transmutation of gold. In fact, he cites
the protagonists of this theory as stating that although they
realize fully the implications or possibilities of such transmutation they have not "proceeded to the praxis". And from
this Mr. Waite utters with attendant disparagements that
such a feat is impossible.

While fully conscious of the philosophic implications
of the spiritual interpretation of the alchemical theory in
so far as it relates to transmutation, I join my predecessors
in confessing that I too have not proceeded to the practice.
But at the same time I am aware of the research and development which has taken place in the past and is proceeding
contemporaneously in modern laboratories. The evidence
of psychical research is material which it would be unwise
for any critic to ignore, let alone ridicule. The various
phenomena which do occur, and whose accuracy and
verisimilitude has been vouched for and attested by honour-
able and trustworthy men, indicates that within man are
strange and wonderful powers but rarely active in the normal
individual. Not only so, but that these psychic factors are able

to affect and influence the objective world to an extraordinary degree. Consider, for example, the phenomenon of
apports. Objects, living and inorganic, make their appearance in the séance-room out of the blue. It seems as if the
magical power activated within the medium is able to
transplant objects in complete disregard of the laws of the
three-dimensional world with which we are familiar, and to
which we have become accustomed. How can we explain
this phenomenon? Flowers are whirled into a room, closed,
locked, and barred—apparently through the floor, ceiling,
or the four walls from somewhere exterior to that room.
Whatever the true explanation, we are face to face with
powers of the psyche which may act upon so-called solid
matter and change and modify its nature solely by psychic
activity. In the face of the vast body of testimony collected
by psychical research, quite apart from spiritualism, we may
say that any individual who ignores such testimony is one
who is a coward intellectually, afraid to accept any truth
which does not conform to his predilections.

This is one aspect of the subject. The other aspect may be
less acceptable to critics, though its validity is attested to by
vast numbers of individuals, and by tradition, secular and
religious. In the Eastern spiritual philosophies it is a commonplace that devotion to the religious life, or the practice
of spiritual techniques, quite definitely develops abnormal
powers in the psyche. These are known in India as the
Siddhis. Legend is rife as to the miracles, so-called, that may
be achieved by fakirs, anchorites, and Yogis. Most of these
with whom the average tourist comes into contact are
manifestly hardly spiritual types. But for the purpose of our
argument that hardly matters. These individuals have
followed the primary rule of occult practice. By doing
certain things, certain results will follow. This rule they have
followed, and have achieved a certain control over mind and
body, developing an enormous potential of will which is
capable of acting directly upon material things. Such a
philosophy of psychism, extended considerably so as to include spiritual development, is the only one which will
explain the miracles of Scripture. Most Western theologians,
unable to explain these phenomena, and incapable of accepting them in the face of scientific criticism, have thrown them

overboard, thus interfering very considerably with biblical narrative and verisimilitude. By adopting the philosophy of Yoga, or any allied or similar art, we have a complete explanation to hand. Through the pursuit of a specialized and scientific study of the psyche, in various of its branches which are not included in modern psychological knowledge, the awakening spirit within manifests through the personality undreamt-of faculties and powers. The exercise of these spiritual powers are responsible for the miracles of both the Old and New Testaments and the scriptures of the East. Moreover, I suggest the interested reader consult Hereward Carrington's excellent work on the psychic life of Christ entitled *Loaves and Fishes*.

In view of both these lines of evidence, the Yoga philosophy of India and modern psychical research, I see on theoretical grounds no valid reason why the interior psychical or magical power should not be able to effect a physical transmutation. If this power can move a physical object without physical contact; if it can exude its own subjective astral substance into objective materialization; if, finally, it can pass one solid object through another without injury or damage to either, why then should it not be able to rearrange the atomic structure of a metal? Theoretically, there is no reason why it should not be so, and I feel confident that, although I have not proceeded to the practice thereof, the future will demonstrate and confirm the truth of what these ancient students have affirmed. In doing so, it will rout with dishonour carping and over-critical students who, because of their long study and supposed insight into the subject, should know better. It is time that such were silenced.

CHAPTER EIGHT

THE MAGICAL VIEW

WE have so far considered the most important theories concerning the non-metallurgical aspect of Alchemy. It must be admitted that the psychological and the magnetic theories are the most important and yield the most significant material. Yet there is a third viewpoint which is worth consideration here—I refer to the magical theory. It touches so closely on the alchemical practice that to ignore it would be to neglect a highly informative branch of research. In other of my works I have dealt fully, more or less, with the objects and nature of magical practices. It may be remarked that from the widest point of view the psychological approach borders very closely on the magical one. As Jung remarks in his commentary to *The Secret of the Golden Flower* :

> Magical practices are the projections of psychic events which, in cases like these, exert a counter influence on the soul and act like a kind of enchantment of one's own personality. That is to say, by means of these concrete performances the attention, or, better said, the interest, is brought back to an inner sacred domain which is the source and goal of the soul. This inner domain contains the unity of life and consciousness which, though once possessed, has been lost and must now be found again.

Thus the objects of Magic are to bring the student to an awareness of his own divine nature, to enable him consciously to integrate and unite the several constituents of his own psyche. It is to effect psychological integration, to bring about a psychic release from bondage to unconscious projection, and to produce an exaltation of consciousness to the Light, that any legitimate magical initiating system owes its existence. The function of every phase of its routine, the avowed intention of its principal rituals, and the explicit statement of its teachings is to assist the candidate by his aspiration to find that unity of being which is the Inner Self, the pure essence of Mind, the Buddha-nature. Thus the entire object of Magic and all mystical training "is, by the intervention of the symbol, ceremonial and sacrament, so to lead the soul that it may be withdrawn from the attraction of matter and delivered from the absorption therein, whereby it walks in somnambulism, knowing not whence it cometh nor whither it goeth".

All magical initiations require the presence of initiating officers. From one point of view such officers represent just such psychic projections as Jung refers to. They represent, even as figures in dreams do, different aspects of man himself, personifications of psychological principles active within the psyche. Through the admittedly artificial or conventional means of a dramatic projection of these psychic principles in a well-ordered ceremony a reaction is induced in consciousness. This reaction is calculated to arouse from their dormant condition those hitherto latent faculties represented objectively by the officers. Without the least conscious effort on the part of the candidate an involuntary current of sympathy is produced by the external delineation of psychic faculties which may be sufficient to accomplish the purpose of the ceremony. The aesthetic appeal to the imagination, quite apart from what I would call the intrinsic magical virtue of the ceremonial, stirs to renewed activity the life of the inner domain. And the entire action of this type of dramatic initiatory ritual is that the soul may discover itself whirled in exaltation to the heights, and during that mystical elevation receive the influx of the Light.

Thus, to refer to one practical magical scheme practised in the Order of the Golden Dawn, and described at length in my book *My Rosicrucian Adventure*, there is a preliminary ritual called the Neophyte Grade. To operate this properly, several officers are required. The Kerux personifies the reasoning faculties. He is the intelligent part of the mind, functioning in obedience to the Will; the Qabalistic *Ruach*, in a word. The higher part of that mind, the aspiring, sensitive, and the intuitive consciousness, the *Neschamah*, is represented by the Hegemon, who ever seeks the rising of the Light. The active will of man is signified by the Hiereus, the guardian against evil. In this initial ceremony of Neophyte the Hierophant acts on behalf of the higher spiritual soul of man himself, that divine self of which but too rarely, if ever at all, we become aware. "The essence of mind is intrinsically pure" is a definition of one Buddhist sutra, and it is this essential state of enlightenment, this interior Self, Osiris glorified through trial and perfected by suffering, which is represented by the Hierophant on the dais. He is seated on the throne of the East in the place of the rising Sun, and with but two or three exceptions never moves from that station in the Temple. He represents that innermost core of the psyche which, itself, moves not, though it directs the other officers and initiates, and commands movement and activity. From his aloof spiritual stronghold this higher Genius gazes down upon its alter-ego, terrestrial man, evolved for the object of providing it with experience. Seldom does that Genius leave its palace of the stars except when, voluntarily, the lower self opens itself to the higher by an act of sincerest aspiration or self-sacrifice, which alone makes possible the descent of the Light within the heart and mind.

Now, it is upon the Hierophant and his activity that the efficacy of initiation depends. Without an understanding of the magnetic theory, no likelihood of realizing the rationale of initiation is possible. The central factor of initiation consists in the communication of spiritual power from the Hierophant to the candidate by a physical and magnetic contact. There is one point in the ceremony when the Hierophant leaves the Throne of the East, representing the Higher Self in action. As Osiris he marks the active descent of the supernal splendour. While leaving the dais, with wand uplifted, he utters : "I come in the power of the Light. I come in the Light of Wisdom. I come in the Mercy of the Light. The Light hath Healing in its Wings." And having brought the Light symbolically to the aspirant, he retires to his throne, as though that divine Genius of whom he is the Temple surrogate and representative awaits the deliberate willing return of the aspirant himself to the everlasting abode of the Light.

In actual practice, in modern times, most Hierophants

have contented themselves solely with the symbolic gesture and speeches. The real significance of the movement, as a practical magnetic technique, has not suggested itself to them. In point of fact, whilst moving from the dais towards the candidate at the altar, the Hierophant should be stirring up within himself the magical or spiritual power to such an extent that it emanates powerfully from him. There are means and techniques by which this is possible. Such are the Middle Pillar technique, the assumption of God-forms, rhythmic breathing, simple but sincere aspiration, prayer, and many another method. The emanation of the spirit entering the sphere of the candidate produces, should the charge be strong enough, a powerful effect.

There is another point, just previous to the one mentioned above, when the Hierophant stands at the altar facing the kneeling Neophyte. Whilst the latter aspires strongly by the recitation of an obligation defining his purpose and intention, the Hierophant takes hold of his left hand. It is this action which, in my estimation, constitutes the principal gesture of successful initiation. For it is then that the Hierophant is able, if he knows his business, to transfer a vital stream of spiritual energy from himself along a physical line of conduction to the candidate.

Now, it is here that we have an analogy to the Atwood conception of alchemical practice. We have seen that the primary operation in Alchemy, regardless of the mode of interpretation, is the solution. According to the Atwood theory, such a solution was accomplished by means of the transference of magnetism or spiritual energy from operator to subject. This transference induced a trance state in the subject. That is, by this means a specific change is induced in consciousness The resemblance of this theory to the action of the Hierophant in magical initiation is at once striking. There is one marked difference however ; no trance state is produced by the ceremony itself. On the other hand, quite frequently the candidate at such initiations confesses afterwards to a sense of confusion or "muzziness", as though some degree of separation, or inhibition of consciousness, had been induced.

Moreover, the action of this Neophyte ceremony is intended—so runs the rubric attached to the ritual—

deliberately to produce a species of schizophrenia. It is believed that the various principles comprising man become temporarily dissociated. A highly intricate account of the condition of these dissociated psychic functions may be found in Volume III of my work *The Golden Dawn*, section Z.3.

So striking is the resemblance of the Atwood technique to the magical one that I am profoundly convinced that the magnetic interpretation, when raised to a higher level and developed to its highest magnitude, is at the basis of ceremonial initiation. Thus the preliminary Neophyte ritual has a definite connection with the Alchemical dissolution. And like that operation of dissolution, upon the efficacy of that Neophyte initiation ceremony does the success of the remaining initiations depend. Should the Hierophant be successful in communicating, with the help of his fellow officers, a magnetic or spiritual charge to the candidate, that charge acts as a ferment. Slowly but surely in the months ensuing after the ceremony the vital ferment stirs up the psyche of the aspirant, unconsciously breaking down resistances and crystallizations, to the end that Light may enter his mind.

The five grades that follow have as their object the awakening of the elemental bases of what must develop into the instrument of the higher. Awakened and purified, they may be consecrated to the Great Work that they may become worthy vehicles for the indwelling of the Light. First, however, it is necessary that they be awakened. For, psychological truism that it is, until their presence is divined their transmutation cannot be accomplished. We have here, again, a definite point of contact with the hermetic technique. For after the dissolution of the inner psychic vehicle into its own homogeneous base there must follow the conversion of the elements. This process, as we assumed before, implies a process of becoming aware of them. The importance and significance of this step becomes imperious if we define the elements as fundamental levels of the Unconscious aspect of the psyche, the broadest divisions of its structure. Once more the magical technique links up with the psychological method. For both aim, though by different methods, at eliminating resistance, and in making conscious the vast inspiration, dynamic energy, and memory concealed in the deeper portions of man's psyche. In symbolic form and pageantry, therefore, the initiation ceremony of each grade calls forth the spirits of a particular element. And as a steel placed in close proximity to a magnet receives some degree of its magnetism, and comparable to the electrical phenomenon of induction, so the presence of power induces power. Contact with the appropriate type of elemental force produces an identical type of reaction within the sphere of the Neophyte, and it is thus that growth and advancement proceeds.

The element offered for the work of transmutation in the grade of Zelator is the earthy part of the Candidate. Here is the beginning of the alchemical conversion of the elements. The ritual symbolically admits him to the first rung of that mighty ladder whose heights are lost in the Light above. The first rung is the lowest sphere of the conventional Tree of Life, *Malkus*. To it is ascribed the first grade and the element of Earth. After the Earth elementals are invoked the Candidate is ceremonially conducted to three stations, the first two being those of evil and the higher divine presence. At each of these Stations the Guardians reject him at the point of the sword, strongly urging him in his unprepared state to return whence he came. His third attempt to go forward places him in a balanced position, the path of equilibrium, the Middle Way, where he is received. And a way is cleared for him by the Hierophant who again represents the celestial soul of things. During his stay in the Temple the stability of the element is established within his consciousness, that eventually it may prove an enduring temple of the Holy Spirit.

The grade after the Earth Ceremony is that of Theoricus. It is referred to the ninth Sephirah on the Tree, *Yesod*, the foundation, and to it are attributed the sphere of the operation of Luna and the reflection of the element Air. Here the candidate is conducted to the stations of the four *Kerubim*, the Angelic choir of Yesod. The Kerubim are defined by Macgregor Mathers in his *Qabalah Unveiled* as the presidents of the elemental forces, the vivified powers of the letters of Tetragrammaton operating in and through the four elements. Each element is by this system of attributions ruled by a Kerub under the aegis of one of the letters of YHVH, the

Ineffable Name. It is always through the power and authority and zodiacal symbol of the Kerub that the elemental spirits and their rulers are invoked. At this juncture of the ceremony with the Airy elements vibrating about and through him, the Zelator is urged to be

> prompt and active as the Sylphs, but avoid frivolity and caprice. Be energetic and strong as the Salamanders, but avoid irritability and ferocity. Be flexible and attentive to images, like the Undines, but avoid idleness and changeability. Be laborious and patient like the Gnomes, but avoid grossness and avarice. So shalt thou gradually develop the powers of thy soul, and fit thyself to command the spirits of the elements.

The third grade is that of Practicus referred to the Sephirah *Hod*, Splendour, the lowest of the left-hand *Sephiros* on the Tree, the so-called Pillar of Severity. Its attributions refer to the sphere of the operation of the Planet Mercury, but more especially to the element of Water which is invoked to power and presence. Two paths lead to this sphere of Splendour—the path of Fire from *Malkus* and the reflection of the sphere of the Sun from *Yesod*. (For clarification of the idea of the Paths between the *Sephiros*, the reader must be referred to my book *A Garden of Pomegranates*.) Water is germinative and maternal, whilst fire is paternal and fructifying ; from their interior stimulation and union is the higher life born even as has been said, "Except ye be baptised with water and the Spirit ye cannot enter the Kingdom of Heaven." Therefore in this grade the Candidate's sphere, symbolized by stagnant water, is by the presence of solar and fiery elements vitalized and rendered a perfect creative base. The emotional life, through the impact of the elemental initiations and contacts, thus becomes enormously stimulated, and a terrific impetus is communicated to the Unconscious psyche.

The fourth grade of Philosophus carries the candidate another step forward. The Sephirah involved is *Netzach*, Victory, to which is referred the operation of the Planet Venus and the element of Fire, while the paths that connect to the lower rungs of the ladder are principally of a

watery nature. Thus the elements ceremonially encountered are of an identical nature with those of the preceding
grade. Here, however, their order and power is totally
reversed. Previously the Water was predominant. Now the
Fire rages and whirls in lurid storm, with Water only as the
complementary element whereon, or through which, it may
reveal itself, and in order that due equilibrium may be
maintained. These two are the primary terrestrial elements
which, intelligently controlled and creatively employed, may
lead eventually to the restoration of the Golden Age. And
by their transmutation a new paradise may be recreated
from the darkness and chaos into which it formerly had
fallen. For the Light may not legitimately be called forth
upon man nor dwell within him until chaos has been turned
into equilibrium or complete realization and enlightenment.
And until order has been restored to the lower elements of
his earthly kingdom neither peace nor inner security may be
his rightful lot.

Though Fire and Water, warmth and moisture, feeling
and emotion raised to their maximum intensity are essentially creative, their stimulation within the being of the
Neophyte draws his attention, perhaps for the first time, to the
chaotic condition of his natural existence, and the complete
psychic muddle into which his ignorance and spiritual
impotence have stranded him. Evocative of the highest
within his soul, equally these elements call forth that which
is base and low, those parts of himself which because of undue
repression have grown revengeful and cruel. The first steps
in the magical work, as in alchemy, are analytical—the
levelling down of all that man formerly held true and holy.
An unhappy state but a very necessary one if progress is to
be made and if the chaos is to be transcended. From these
ruins may be erected the new temple of Light ; it is always
from the rubbish heap that are selected the materials for the
manifestation of god-head. These symbols have a dual
application. Not only do they refer to the epochs of creative
evolution whose memory has long since faded even from the
visible memory of Nature, but also to the recapitulation of
those periods within consciousness itself. And it is in connection with these recapitulations that "the aspirant on the
threshold of Initiation", observes Aleister Crowley, "finds

himself assailed by the 'complexes' which have corrupted him, their externalization excruciating him, and his agonized reluctance to their elimination plunging him into such ordeals that he seems (both to himself and to others) to have turned from a noble and upright man into an unutterable scoundrel". These are the experiences and events which occur to every aspirant when initiation forces the realization upon him that "all is sorrow". In fact, the hallmark of successful initiation and alchemical practice would seem to lie in the occurrence of these or similar experiences —the increased awareness of conflict. The whole universe under the stimulation of the magical elements and inward analysis seems to tumble like a pack of cards crazily about one's feet. This is the first half of the alchemical *solvé et coagula* formula. Analysis or dissolution must precede synthesis. Corruption is the primitive base from which the pure gold of the spirit is drawn. So far as the nature of the environment and personal understanding and creative capacity permit, the task implied by the *coagula* formula is to assemble them and remould them nearer to the heart's desire.

The Philosophus grade completes the four elemental initiations. In the candidate's consciousness have been implanted the seeds of Earth, Air, Fire, and Water, and thus the alchemical conversion of the elements has been accomplished. As explained on a former page, the magical philosophy postulates a fifth element which acts as the Quintessence or synthesis of the other four. Following the Fire grade, therefore, comes the Grade of the Portal. This conferred upon the candidate the title of the Lord of the Paths of the Portal of the Vault of the Adepti, and is not referred to any Sephirah as such. Its technical attribution is the element of *Akasa*, Spirit or Ether. It is intermediate between the elemental grades and the higher spiritual attainments beyond. A crown to the four lower elements, the Rite formulates above Earth, Air, Water, and Fire, the uppermost point of the Pentagram, revealing the administration of the Light over and through the kingdom of the natural world. It concerns itself with a recapitulation of the former grades, co-ordinating and equilibriating the elemental self which, symbolically sacrificed upon the mystic altar, is offered to the service of the higher Genius. Not only does this Grade concern itself with the Quintessence or the Mercury of the Philosophers, but it carries the alchemical procedure a step further, providing another definite similarity to the hermetic technique. The Second and Third Adepts, two of the initiating officers, bear in their hands wands which are surmounted by alchemical symbols. The former represents the principle of Sulphur, whilst the latter represents Salt. The Hierophant, or Chief Adept as he is named at this stage, bears a wand marked to represent all three principles of Mercury, Sulphur and Salt. The grade then clearly corresponds to a stage in the alchemical Art. Not only is the concept of the Quintessence developed in so far as it is the synthesis of the four elements, but it is taught that within it are concealed the Three Alchemical Principles. The functions of the higher grades must be then to develop these principles, to separate them from their base, and to become fully and consciously aware of their implicits.

A gestation period of at least nine months elapsed prior to initiation to the Adeptus Minor grade, a grade which is excessively difficult to describe except by quotation from the Ritual concerned. Its function explains itself in these terms : "Buried with that Light in a mystical death, rising again in a mystical resurrection, cleansed and purified through him our Master, O brother of the Cross of the Rose. Like him O Adepts of all ages have ye toiled ; like him have ye suffered tribulation. Poverty, torture, and death have ye passed through. They have been but the purification of the Gold. In the alembic of thine heart, through the athanor of affliction, seek thou the true stone of the wise."

The chief characteristic of this grade is that it marks at least symbolically the attainment of a distinct phase of spiritual realization. In a fascinating and extremely brilliant way, the entire structure of the ritual emphasizes and connives to induce this phenomenon. At one juncture of the ceremony, the candidate is affixed to a large upstanding Cross. Thereon under the most solemn circumstances he is obliged to assume a sacred vow. The officiating adept reads several phrases first, and the candidate repeats them. It is not difficult to realize that this is a difficult and important phase of the Ceremony. During this obligation because of the symbolism attached to it, and because of the active aspiration which is induced at this stage, illumination may quite easily occur, and very often does. Provided, naturally, that the officers fulfil their part. The object of the ceremony as a whole "is especially intended to effect the change of the consciousness into the *Neschamah*, and there are three places where this can take place. The first is when the aspirant is on the Cross, because he is so exactly fulfilling the symbol of the abnegation of the lower self and the Union with the Higher Self". Suffice to mention that he is now entitled to undertake a definite magical training after this grade, a training which comprises instruction in the art of meditation, visualization, assumption of God-forms, awakening of the inner psycho-physical centres or chakras, etc. It is un-necessary here to give further details of the magical rituals ; interested readers will discover full details in *My Rosicrucian Adventure* and *The Golden Dawn*.

Thus, the entire direction of Magic is more than com-parable to Alchemy. Both lead from a dissolution of the psychic crystallizations by the light and power of the spirit towards a free and active manifestation of the spiritual self. Being "brought to the Light" is a very apposite description of the great Work. This experience of the rising of the Light is common to mystics of every age and of every people. It is an experience of the greatest significance, a goal marking an attainment, the achievement of a distinct evolution. It is an ineffable experience, however, which defies definition, as well in its elementary flashes as in its most advanced transports. No code of thought, philosophy or religion, no logical process can bind or limit it. Always does it represent, spiritually, a marked attainment, a liberation from the perplexing turmoil of life, from conflict, and from every psychic complication. As Jung has expressed it, it "thereby frees the inner personality from emotional and imaginary entanglements, creating thus a unity of being which is universally felt as a release". It is the attainment of spiritual puberty, a significant stage in spiritual growth, marking the proper concoction of that precious gem, the Stone of the Wise, and fulfilling the complete transmutation of the bodily lead into the gold of full soul-realization in consciousness.

BOOK THREE

CHAPTER NINE

COELUM TERRAE

Or The Magician's Heavenly Chaos.
By Thomas Vaughan.*

I HAVE now, Reader, performed my promise and—according to my *posse*—proved the antiquity of magic. I am not so much a fool as to expect a general subscription to my endeavours. Every man's *placet* is not the same with mine ; but "the die is cast". I have done this much, and he that will overthrow it must know, in the first place, it is his task to do more. There is one point I can justly bind an adversary to—that he shall not oppose man to God, heathen romances to Divine Scriptures. He that would foil me must use such weapons as I do, for I have not fed my readers with straw, neither will I be confuted with stubble. In the next place, it is my design to speak something of the Art itself, and this I shall do in rational terms, a form different from the ancients; for I will not stuff my discourse like a wilderness with lions and dragons. To common philosophers that fault is very proper which Quintilian observed in some orators : "The summits of their structures are in evidence ; the foundations are hidden." The spires of their Babel are in the clouds, its fundamentals nowhere. They talk indeed of fine things but tell us not upon what grounds. To avoid these flights, I shall in this my *olla*—for I care not much what I shall call it—observe this composition. First, I shall speak of that one only

---

*Thomas Vaughan was born in Llansaintffraid on the banks of the Usk in 1621. His brother Henry Vaughan the poet is rather better known than he is. This book was published for Thomas Vaughan in 1650 by H. Blunden at the Castle in Cornhill. Mr. A. E. Waite has produced an edition of all Vaughan's writings, including the present text, in one volume. *Coelum Terrae* is an excellent specimen of his work, besides being a very fine example of one kind of alchemical writing.

thing which is the subject of this Art and the mother of all things. Secondly, I will discourse of that most admirable and more than natural Medicine which is generated out of this one thing. Lastly—though with some disorder—I will discover the means how and by which this Art works upon the subject ; but these being the keys which lead to the very *estrado* of Nature, where she sits in full solemnity and receives the visits of the philosophers, I must scatter them in several parts of the discourse. This is all, and here thou must not consider how long or short I shall be but how full the discovery ; and truly it shall be such and so much that thou canst not in modesty expect more.

Now then, you that would be what the ancient physicians were, "the health-giving hands of the gods", not quacks and salvos of the pipkin ; you that would perform what you publicly profess and make your callings honest and conscionable : attend to the truth without spleen. Remember that prejudice is no religion and by consequence hath no reward. If this Art were damnable you might safely study it notwithstanding, for you have a precept to "prove all things" but to "hold fast that which is good". It is your duty not to be wanting to yourselves ; and for my part—that I may be wanting to none—thus I begin.

Said the Kabalist : "The building of the Sanctuary which is here below is framed according to that of the Sanctuary which is above." Here we have two worlds, visible and invisible, and two universal Natures, visible and invisible, out of which both those worlds proceeded. The passive universal Nature was made in the image of the active universal one, and the conformity of both worlds or Sanctuaries consists in the original conformity of their principles. There are many Platonics—and this last century hath afforded them some apish disciples—who discourse very boldly of the similitudes of inferiors and superiors ; but if we thoroughly search their trash· it is a pack of small conspiracies—namely, of the heliotrope and the sun, iron and the lodestone, the wound and the weapon. It is excellent sport to hear how they crow, being roosted on these pitiful particulars, as if they knew the universal magnet which binds this great frame and moves all the members of it to a mutual compassion. This is an humour much like that of Don Quixote, who knew Dulcinea but never saw her. Those students then who would be better instructed must first know there is an universal agent, Who when He was disposed to create had no other pattern or exemplar whereby to frame and mould His creatures but Himself. But having infinite inward ideas or conceptions in Himself, as He conceived so He created : that is to say, He created an outward form answerable to the inward conception or figure of His mind. In the second place, they ought to know there is an universal patient, and this passive Nature was created by the Universal Agent. This general patient is the immediate catholic character of God Himself in His Unity and trinity. In plain terms it is that substance which we commonly call the First Matter. But verily it is to no purpose to know this notion (or) Matter unless we know the thing itself to which the notion relates. We must see it, handle it and by experimental ocular demonstration know the very central invisible essences and properties of it. But of these things hear the most excellent Capnion, who informs his Jew and his Epicure of two catholic natures—material and spiritual.

One nature (saith he) is such it may be seen with the eyes and felt with the hands, and it is subject to alteration almost in every moment. You must pardon— as Apuleius saith—this strange expression, because it makes for the obscurity of the thing. This very nature— since she may not continue one and the same—is notwithstanding apprehended of the mind under her such qualification more rightly as she is than as she is not, namely, as the thing itself is in truth—that is to say, changeable. The other nature or principle of substances is incorruptible, immutable, constant, one and the same for ever, and always existent.

Thus he. Now, this changeable nature whereof he speaks is the first, visible, tangible substance that ever God made : it is white in appearance and Paracelsus gives you the reason why : "All things," saith he, "when they first proceed from God are white, but He colours them afterwards according to His pleasure." An example we have in this very matter, which the philosophers call sometimes their Red Magnesia, sometimes their white, by which descriptions they have deceived many men. For in the first preparation the chaos is blood-red, because the Central Sulphur is stirred up and discovered by the Philosophical Fire. In the second it is exceeding white and transparent like the heavens. It is in truth somewhat like common quicksilver, but of a celestial, transcendent brightness, for there is nothing upon earth like it. This fine substance is the child of the elements and it is a most pure sweet virgin, for nothing as yet hath been generated out of her. But if at any time she breeds it is by the fire of Nature, for that is her husband. She is no animal, no vegetable, no mineral, neither is she extracted out of animals, vegetables or minerals, but she is pre-existent to them all, for she is the mother of them. Yet one thing I must say : she is not much short of life, for she is almost animal. Her composition is miraculous and different from all other compounds whatsoever. Gold is not so compact but every sophister concludes it is no simple ; but she is so much one that no man believes she is more. She yields to nothing but love, for her end is generation and that was never yet performed by violence. He that knows how to wanton and toy with her, the same shall receive all her treasures. First, she sheds at her nipples a thick, heavy water, but white as any snow : the philosophers call it Virgin's Milk. Secondly, she gives him blood from her very heart : it is a quick, heavenly fire ; some improperly call it their sulphur. Thirdly and lastly, she presents him with a secret crystal, of more worth and lustre than the white rock and all her rosials. This is she, and these are her favours : catch her, if you can.

To this character and discovery of my own I shall add some more descriptions, as I find her limned and dressed by her other lovers. Some few—but such as knew her very well—have written that she is not only one and three but withal four and five, and this truth is essential. The titles they have bestowed on her are diverse. They call her their Catholic Magnesia and the Sperm of the World out of which all natural things are generated. Her birth—say they—is singular and not without a miracle, her complexion heavenly and different from her parents. Her body also in some sense is incorruptible and the common elements cannot destroy it, neither will she mix with them essentially. In the outward shape or figure she resembles a stone and yet is no stone, for they call her their White Gum and Water of the Sea, Water of Life, Most Pure and Blessed Water ; and yet they mind not water of the clouds or rain water, nor water of the well, nor dew, but a certain thick, permanent, saltish water, that is dry and wets not the hands, a viscous, slimy water generated out of the fatness of the earth. They call her also their twofold Mercury and Azoth, begotten by the influences of two globes, celestial and terrestrial. Moreover, they affirm her to be of that nature that no fire can destroy her, which of all other descriptions is most true, for she is fire herself, having in her a portion of the universal fire of Nature and a secret celestial spirit, which spirit is animated and quickened by God Himself, wherefore also they call her their Most Blessed Stone. Lastly, they say she is a middle nature between thick and thin, neither altogether earthy nor altogether fiery but a mean aerial substance—to be found everywhere and every time of the year.

This is enough. But that I may speak something myself in plain terms, I say she is a very salt, but extreme soft and somewhat thin and fluid, not so hard, not so thick as common extracted salts, for she is none of them, nor any kind of salt whatsoever that man can make. She is a sperm that Nature herself draws out of the elements without the help of art. Man may find it where Nature leaves it ; it is not of his office to make the sperm, nor to extract it. It is already made and wants nothing but a matrix and heat convenient for generation. Now should you consider with yourselves where Nature leaves the seed, and yet many are so dull they know not how to work when they are told what they must do. We see in animal generations the sperm parts not from both the parents, for it remains with the female, where it is perfected. In the great world, though all the elements contribute to the composure of the sperm yet the sperm parts not from all the elements but remains with the earth or with the water though more immediately with the one than with the other. Let not your thoughts feed now on the phlegmatic, indigested vomits of Aristotle ; look on the green, youthful and flowery bosom of the earth. Consider what a vast universal receptacle this element is. The stars and planets overlook her and—though they may not descend hither themselves—

they shed down their golden locks, like so many bracelets and tokens of love. The sun is perpetually busy, brings his fire round about her, as if he would sublime something from her bosom and rob her of some secret, enclosed jewel. Is there anything lost since the creation ? Wouldst thou know his very bed and his pillow ? It is earth. How many cities, dost thou think, have perished with the sword ? How many by earthquakes ? And how many by the deluge ? Thou dost perhaps desire to know where they are at this present : believe it, they have one common sepulchre. What was once their mother is now their tomb. All things return to that place from whence they came, and that very place is earth. If thou hast but leisure, run over the alphabet of Nature ; examine every letter—I mean every particular creature— in her book. What becomes of her grass, her corn, her herbs, her flowers ? True it is, both man and beast do use them, but this only by the way, for they rest not till they come to earth again. In this element they had their first and in this will they have their last station. Think—if other vanities will give thee leave—on all those generations that went be- fore thee and anticipate all those that shall come after thee. Where are those beauties the times past have produced and what will become of those that shall appear in future ages ? They will all to the same dust ; they have one common house ; and there is no family so numerous as that of the grave. Do but look on the daily sports of Nature, her clouds and mists, the scene and pageantry of the air. Even these momentary things retreat to the closet of the earth. If the sun makes her dry she can drink as fast ; what gets up in clouds comes down in water ; the earth swallows up all and like that philosophical dragon eats her own tail. The wise poets saw this and in their mystical language called the earth Saturn, telling us withal she did feed on her own children. Verily, there is more truth in their stately verse than in Aristotle's dull prose, for he was a blind beast and malice made him so.

But to proceed a little further with you, I wish you to concoct what you read, to dwell a little upon earth, not to fly up presently and admire the meteors of your own brains. The earth, you know, in the winter-time is a dull, dark, dead thing—a contemptible, frozen, phlegmatic lump. But towards the spring and fomentations of the sun what rare pearls are there in this dung-hill, what glorious colours and tinctures doth she discover ! A pure, eternal green overspreads her, and this attended with innumerable other beauties—roses red and white, golden lilies, azure violets, the bleeding hyacinths, with their several celestial odours and spices. If you will be advised by me, learn from whence the earth hath these invisible treasures, this annual flora, which appears not without the compliments of the sun. Behold, I will tell you as plainly as I may. There are in the world two extremes—matter and spirit. One of these, I can assure you, is earth. The influences of the spirit animate and quicken the matter, and in the material extreme the seed of the spirit is to be found. In middle natures—as fire, air, and water—this seed stays not, for they are but *dispenseros* or *media*, which convey it from one extreme to the other, from the spirit to the matter—that is, the earth. But stay, my friend ; this intelligence hath somewhat stirred you, and now you come on so furiously, as if you would rifle the cabinet. Give me leave to put you back. I mind not this common, feculent, impure earth ; that falls not within my discourse, but as it makes for your manuduction. That which I speak of is a mystery : it is *coelum terrae* and *terrae coeli*, not this dirt and dust but a most secret, celestial, invisible earth.

Raymund Lully, in his *Compendium of Alchemy*, calls the principles of art magic "certain fugitive spirits, condensed in the air, in the shape of divers monsters, beasts and men, which move like clouds hither and thither". As for the sense of our Spaniard, I refer it to his readers ; let them make the most of it.

This is true ; as the air and all the volatile substances in it are restless, even so is it with the First Matter. The eye of man never saw her twice under one and the same shape ; but as clouds driven by the wind are forced to this and that figure—but cannot possibly retain one constant form—so is she persecuted by the fire of Nature. For this fire and this water are like two lovers : they no sooner meet but presently they play and toy, and this game will not over till some new baby is generated. I have oftentimes admired their subtle perpetual motion, for at all times and in all places these two are busy, which occasioned that notable sentence

of Trismegistus', that action was the life of God. But most
excellent and magisterial is that oracle of Marcus Antoninus,
who in his discourse to himself speaks indeed things worthy
of himself. "The nature," saith he, "of the universe delights
not in anything so much as to alter all things and then to
make the like again." This is her tick-tack : she plays one
game, to begin another. The Matter is placed before her like
a piece of wax, and she shapes it to all forms and figures.
Now she makes a bird, now a beast, now a flower, then a
frog, and she is pleased with her own magical performances
as men are with their own fancies. Hence she is called of
Orpheus "the mother that makes many things and ordains
strange shapes or figures". Neither doth she as some sinful
parents do, who—having their pleasure—care not for their
child. She loves them still after she hath made them, hath
an eye over them all and provides even for her sparrows.
'Tis strange to consider that she works as well privately as
publicly, not only in gardens, where ladies may smell her
perfumes, but in remote solitudes and deserts. The truth is
she seeks not to please others so much as herself, wherefore
many of her works—and those the choicest—never come to
light.

We see little children, who are newly come from under
her hand, will be dabbling in dirt and water, and other idle
sports affected by none but themselves. The reason is they
are not as yet captivated, which makes them seek their own
pleasures. But when they come to age then love or profit
makes them square their actions according to other men's
desires. Some cockney claps his revenue on his back, but his
gallantry is spoiled if his mistress doth not observe it. Another
fights, but his victory is lost if it be not printed ; it is the
world must hear of his valour. Now, Nature is a free spirit
that seeks no applause ; she observes none more than
herself but is pleased with her own magic, as philosophers
are with their secret philosophy. Hence it is that we find her
busy not only in the pots of the balconies but in wilder-
nesses and ruinous places, where no eyes observe her but the
stars and planets. In a word, wheresoever the fire of Nature
finds the Virgin Mercury there hath he found his love,
and there will they both fall to their husbandry, a pleasure
not subject to surfeits, for it still presents new varieties.

It is reported of Mark Antony, a famous but unfortunate Roman, how he sent his agent over the world to copy all the handsome faces, that amongst so many excellent features he might select for himself the most pleasing piece. Truly Nature is much of this strain, for she hath infinite beauteous patterns in herself, and all these she would gladly see beyond herself, which she cannot do without the Matter—for that is her glass. This makes her generate perpetually and imprint her conceptions in the Matter, communicating life to it and figuring it according to her imagination. By this practice she placeth her fancy or idea beyond herself, or, as the Peripatetics say, beyond the Divine Mind, namely, in the Matter. But the ideas being innumerable and withal different, the pleasures of the agent are maintained by their variety or—to speak more properly—by his own fruitfulness, for amongst all the beauties the world affords there are not two that are altogether the same.

Much might be spoken in this place concerning beauty, what it is, from whence it came, and how it may be defaced, not only in the outward figure but in the inward idea and lost for ever in both worlds. But these pretty shuttles I am no way acquainted with : I have no mistress but Nature, wherefore I shall leave the fine ladies to fine lads and speak of my simple

AElia Laelia

It was scarce day when all alone
I saw Hyanthe and her throne.
In fresh green damask she was dressed
And o'er a sapphire globe did rest.
This slippery sphere when I did see,
Fortune, I thought it had been thee.
But when I saw she did present
A majesty more permanent
I thought my cares not lost if I
Should finish my discovery.

Sleepy she look'd to my first sight,
As if she had watch'd all the night,
And underneath her hand was spread
The white supporter of her head.

But at my second, studied view
I could perceive a silent dew
Steal down her cheeks, lest it should stain
Those cheeks where only smiles should reign.
The tears stream'd down for haste and all
In chains of liquid pearl did fall.
Fair sorrows—and more dear than joys,
Which are but empty airs and noise
Your drops present a richer prize,
For they are something like her eyes.

Pretty white fool, why hast thou been
Sullied with tears and not with sin ?
'Tis true thy tears, like polished skies,
Are the bright rosials of thy eyes ;
But such strange fates do them attend
As if thy woes would never end.
From drops to sighs they turn and then
Those sighs return to drops again ;
But whiles the silver torrent seeks
Those flowers that watch it in thy cheeks
The white and red Hyanthe wears
Turn to rose-water all her tears.

Have you beheld a flame that springs
From incense when sweet curled rings
Of smoke attend her last weak fires,
And she all in perfumes expires ?
So did Hyanthe. Here—said she—
Let not this vial part from thee.
It holds my heart, though now 'tis spill'd
And into waters all distill'd.
'Tis constant still. Trust not false smiles:
Who smiles and weeps not she beguiles.
Nay, trust not tears : false are the few ;
Those tears are many that are true.
Trust me and take the better choice :
Who hath my tears can want no joys.

I know some sophisters of the Heptarchy—I mean those
whose learning is all noise, in which sense even pyannets
and paraquitoes are philosophical—will conclude this all
bait and poetry ; that we are pleasing, not positive, and
cheat even the reader's discretion. To prevent such impotent

calumnies, and to spend a little more of our secret light upon the well-disposed student, I shall in this place produce the testimonics of some able philosophers concerning the First Matter itself, as it is naturally found before any alteration by art. And here verily the reader may discover the mark. It is most easily done, if he will but eye the flights of my verse or follow the more grave pace of their prose. The first I shall cite is Arnoldus de Nova, an absolute perfect master of the Art. He describes the Philosophical Chaos in these plain terms :

> It is (saith he) a stone and no stone, spirit, soul, and body ; which if thou dissolvest, it will be dissolved ; and if thou dost coagulate it, it will be coagulated ; and if thou dost make it fly, it will fly ; for it is volatile or flying and clear as a tear. Afterwards it is made citrine, then saltish ; but without shoots or crystals, and no man may touch it with his tongue. Behold, I have described it truly to thee, but I have not named it. Now I will name it ; and I say that if thou sayest it is water thou dost say the truth ; and if thou sayest it is not water thou dost lie. Be not therefore deceived with manifold descriptions and operations, for it is but one thing, to which nothing extraneous may be added.

Thus Arnoldus, and he borrowed this from the Turba. Let us now hear his disciple Raymund Lully, who, speaking very enviously and obscurely of seven metallic principles, describes the third—wherein four of the seven are included —in these words. Saith he :

> The third principle is a clear, compounded water, and it is the next substance in complexion to quicksilver. It is found running and flowing upon the earth. This quicksilver is generated in every compound out of the substance of the air, and therefore the moisture of it is extreme heavy.

To these I will add Albertus Magnus, whose suffrage in this kind of learning is like the stylanx to gold, for he had thoroughly searched it and knew very well what part of it would abide the test. In plain English saith he :

The Mercury of the wise men is a watery element cold and moist. This is their Permanent Water, the spirit of the body, the unctuous vapour, the blessed water, the virtuous water, the water of the wise men, the philosopher's vinegar, the mineral water, the dew of heavenly grace, the virgin's milk, the bodily Mercury ; and with other numberless names is it named in the books of the philosophers ; which names truly—though they are divers notwithstanding—always signify one and the same thing, namely, the Mercury of the wise men. Out of this Mercury alone all the virtue of the Art is extracted and —according to its nature—the Tincture, both red and white.

To this agrees Rachaidibi, the Persian. "The sperm or First Matter," saith he, "of the stone is outwardly cold and moist but inwardly hot and dry." All which is confirmed by Rhodian, another instructor, it seems, of Kanid, King of Persia. His words are these :

The sperm is white and liquid, afterwards red. This sperm is the Flying Stone, and it is aerial and volatile, cold and moist, hot and dry.

To these subscribes the author of that excellent tract entitled *The Book of the Three Words*.

This (saith he) is the Book of Three Words, meaning thereby Three Principles ; the Book of the Precious Stone, which is a body aerial and volatile, cold and moist, watery and adustive ; and in it is heat and drought, coldness and moisture, one virtue inwardly, the other outwardly.

Belus the philosopher, in that famous and most classic Synod of Arisleus, inverts the order to conceal the practice ; but if rightly understood he speaks to the same purpose.

Amongst all great philosophers (saith he) it is magisterial that our Stone is no stone ; but amongst ignorants it is ridiculous and incredible. For who will believe that water can be made a stone and a stone water, nothing being more different than these two ? And yet in very truth it is so. For this very Permanent Water is the Stone ; but whiles it is water it is no stone.

But in this sense the ancient Hermes abounds and almost discovers too much.

Know (saith he), you that are children of the wise : the separation of the ancient philosophers was performed upon water, which separation divides the water into four other substances.

There is extant a very learned author who hath written something to this purpose, and that more openly than any whom we have formerly cited.

As the world (saith he) was generated out of that Water upon which the Spirit of God did move, all things proceeding thence, both celestial and terrestrial, so this chaos is generated out of a certain Water that is not common, not out of dew nor air condensed in the caverns of the earth, or artificially in the receiver ; not out of water drawn out of the sea, fountains, pits, or rivers; but out of a certain tortured water that hath suffered some alteration. Obvious it is to all but known to very few. This water hath all in it that is necessary to the perfection of the work, without any extrinsical addition.

I could produce a thousand authors more, but that were tedious. I shall conclude with one of the Rosy Brothers, whose testimony is equivalent to the best of these, but his instruction far more excellent. His discourse of the First Matter is somewhat large, and to avoid prolixity I shall forbear the Latin, but I will give thee his sense in punctual, plain English.

I am a goddess (saith he, speaking in the person of Nature), for beauty and extraction famous, born out of our own proper sea which compasseth the whole earth and is ever restless. Out of my breasts I pour forth milk and blood : boil these two till they are turned into silver and gold. O most excellent subject, out of which all things in this world are generated, though at the first sight thou art poison, adorned with the name of the Flying Eagle. Thou are the First Matter, the seed of Divine Benediction, in whose body there is heat and rain, which notwithstanding are hidden from the wicked, because of thy habit and virgin vestures which are scattered over all the world. Thy parents are the sun and moon ; in thee there is water and wine, gold also and silver upon earth, that mortal man may rejoice. After this manner God sends us His blessing and wisdom with rain and the beams of the sun, to the eternal glory of His Name. But consider, O man, what things God bestows upon thee by this means. Torture the Eagle till she weeps and the Lion be weakened and bleed to death. The blood of this Lion, incorporated with the tears of the Eagle, is the treasure of the earth. These creatures use to devour and kill one another, but notwithstanding their love is mutual, and they put on the property and nature of a Salamander, which if it remains in the fire without any detriment it cures all the diseases of men, beasts, and metals. After that the ancient philosophers had perfectly understood this subject they diligently sought in this mystery for the centre of the middlemost tree in the Terrestrial Paradise, entering in by five litigious gates. The first gate was the knowledge of the True Matter, and here arose the first and that a most bitter conflict. The second was the preparation by which this Matter was to be prepared, that they might obtain the embers of the Eagle and the blood of the Lion. At this gate there is a most sharp fight, for it produceth water and blood and a spiritual, bright body. The third gate is the fire which conduceth to the maturity of the Medicine. The fourth gate is that of multiplication and augmentation, in which proportions and weight are necessary. The fifth and last gate is projection. But most glorious, full rich and high is he who attains to the fourth gate, for he hath got an universal Medicine for all diseases. This is that great character of the Book of Nature out of which her whole alphabet doth arise. The fifth gate serves only for metals. This mystery, existing from the foundation of the world and the creation of Adam, is of all others the most ancient, a knowledge which God Almighty—by His Word—breathed into Nature, a miraculous power, the blessed fire of life, the transparent carbuncle and red gold of the wise men, and the Divine Benediction of this life. But this mystery, because of the malice and wickedness of men, is given only to few, notwithstanding it lives and moves every day in the sight of the whole world, as it appears by the following parable.

I am a poisonous dragon, present everywhere and to be had for nothing. My water and my fire dissolve and compound. Out of my body thou shalt draw the Green and the Red Lion ; but if thou dost not exactly know me thou wilt—with my fire—destroy thy five senses. A most pernicious, quick poison comes out of my nostrils which hath been the destruction of many. Separate therefore the thick from the thin artificially, unless thou dost delight in extreme poverty. I give thee faculties both male and female and the powers both of heaven and earth. The mysteries of my art are to be performed magnanimously and with great courage if thou wouldst have me overcome the violence of the fire, in which attempt many have lost both their labour and their substance. I am the egg of Nature known only to the wise such as are pious and modest, who make of me a little world. Ordained I was by the Almighty God for men, but—though many desire me—I am given only to few that they may relieve the poor with my treasures and not set their minds on gold that perisheth. I am called of the philosophers Mercury : my husband is gold philosophical. I am the old dragon that is present everywhere on the face of the earth. I am father and mother, youthful and ancient, weak and yet most strong, life and death, visible and invisible, hard and soft, descending to the earth and ascending to the heavens, most high and most low, light and heavy. In me the order of Nature is oftentimes inverted—in colour, number, weight, and measure. I have in me the light of Nature ; I am dark and bright ; I spring from the earth and I come out of heaven ; I am well known and yet a mere nothing ; all

M

colours shine in me and all metals by the beams of the
sun. I am the Carbuncle of the Sun, a most noble,
clarified earth, by which thou mayst turn copper, iron,
tin, and lead into most pure gold.

Now, gentlemen, you may see which way the philosophers
move : they commend their Secret Water and I admire the
tears of Hyanthe. There is something in the fancy besides
poetry, for my mistress is very philosophical and in her love
a pure platonic. But now I think upon it, how many rivals
shall I procure by this discourse ? Every reader will fall to
and some fine thing may break her heart with nonsense.
This love indeed were mere luck ; but for my part I dare trust
her, and lest any man should mistake her for some things
formerly named I will tell you truly what she is. She is not
any known water whatsoever but a secret spermatic moisture, or rather the Venus that yields that moisture. Therefore do not you imagine that she is any crude, phlegmatic,
thin water, for she is a fat, thick, heavy, slimy humidity.
But lest you should think I am grown jealous and would not
trust you with my mistress, Arnoldus de Villa Nova shall
speak for me : hear him.

I tell thee further (saith he) that we could not
possibly find, neither could the philosophers find before
us, anything that would persist in the fire but only the
unctuous humidity. A watery humidity we see will easily
vapour away, and the earth remains behind, and the
parts are therefore separated because their composition
is not natural. But if we consider those humidities which
are hardly separated from those parts which are natural
to them, we find not any such but the unctuous, viscous
humidities.

It will be expected perhaps by some flint and antimony
doctors—who make their philosophical contrition with a
hammer—that I should discover this thing outright and not
suffer this strange bird-lime to hold their pride by the
plumes. To these I say it is Water of Silver, which some have
called Water of the Moon ; but 'tis Mercury of the Sun, and
partly of Saturn, for it is extracted from these three metals

and without them it can never be made. Now they may unriddle and tell me what it is, for it is truth—if they can understand it.

To the ingenuous and modest reader I have something else to reply, and I believe it will sufficiently excuse me. Raymund Lully—a man who had been in the centre of Nature and without all question understood a great part of the Divine Will—gives me a most terrible charge not to prostitute these principles. Saith he :

I swear to thee upon my soul that thou art damned if thou shouldst reveal these things. For every good thing proceeds from God and to Him only is due. Wherefore thou shalt reserve and keep that secret which God only should reveal, and thou shalt affirm thou dost justly keep back those things whose revelation belongs to His honour. For if thou shouldst reveal that in a few words which God hath been forming a long time, thou shouldst be condemned in the great day of judgment as a traitor to the majesty of God, neither should thy treason be forgiven thee. For the revelation of such things belongs to God and not to man.

So said the wise Raymund.

Now, for my part, I have always honoured the magicians, their philosophy being both rational and majestic, dwelling not upon notions but effects, and those such as confirm both the wisdom and the power of the Creator. When I was a mere errant in their books, and understood them not, I did believe them. Time rewarded my faith and paid my credulity with knowledge. In the interim I suffered many bitter calumnies, and this by some envious adversaries who had nothing of a scholar but their gowns and a little language for vent to their nonsense. But these could not remove me ; with a Spartan patience I concocted my injuries and found at last that Nature was magical, not peripatetical. I have no reason then to distrust them in spiritual things, whom I have found so orthodox and faithful even in natural mysteries. I do believe Raymund, and in order to that faith I provide for my salvation. I will not discover, that I may not be condemned. But if this will not satisfy thee—whoever thou art—let me whisper thee a word in the ear, and afterwards do thou proclaim it on the housetop. Dost thou know from whom and how that sperm or seed which men for want of a better name call the First Matter proceeded ? A certain illuminatee—and in his days a member of that Society which some painted buzzards use to laugh at—writes thus :

God (saith he), incomparably good and great, out of nothing created something ; but that something was made one thing, in which all things were contained, creatures both celestial and terrestrial.

This first something was a certain kind of cloud or darkness, which was condensed into water, and this water is that one thing in which all things were contained. But my question is : What was that nothing out of which the first cloudy chaos or something was made ? Canst thou tell me ? It may be thou dost think it is a mere nothing. It is indeed *nihil quo ad nos*—nothing that we perfectly know. It is nothing, as Dionysius saith : it is nothing that was created or of those things that are and nothing of that which thou dost call nothing—that is, of those things that are not, in thy empty, destructive sense.

But, by your leave, it is the True Thing, of Whom we can affirm nothing. It is that Transcendent Essence Whose theology is negative and was known to the primitive Church but is lost in these our days. This is that nothing of Cornelius Agrippa, and in this nothing when he was tired with human things—I mean human sciences—he did at last rest. "To know nothing is the happiest life." True indeed, for to know this nothing is life eternal. Learn, then, to understand that magical axiom "the visible was formed from the invisible", for all visibles came out of the invisible God, for He is the well-spring whence all things flow, and the creation was a certain stupendous birth or delivery. This fine Virgin Water, or chaos, was the Second Nature from God Himself and—if I may say so—the child of the Blessed Trinity. What doctor, then, is he whose hands are fit to touch that subject upon which God Himself, when He works, lays His own Spirit ? For verily so we read : "The Spirit of God moved upon the face of the water." And can it be expected, then, that I should prostitute this mystery to all hands whatsoever, that I should proclaim it and cry it as they cry oysters? Verily these considerations, with some other which I will not for all the world put to paper, have made me almost displease my dearest friends, to whom, notwithstanding, I owe a better satisfaction. Had it been my fortune barely to know this Matter, as most men do, I had perhaps been less careful of it; but I have been instructed in all the secret circumstances thereof, which few upon earth understand. I speak not for any ostentation, but I speak a truth which my conscience knows very well. Let me, then, Reader, request thy patience, for I shall leave this discovery to God, Who—if it be His blessed will—can call unto thee and say: Here it is and thus I work it.

I had not spoken all this in my own defence had I not been assaulted—as it were—in this very point and told to my face I was bound to discover all that I knew, for this age looks for dreams and revelations as the train to their invisible righteousness. I have now sufficiently discoursed of the Matter, and if it be not thy fortune to find it by what is here written, yet thou canst not be deceived by what I have said, for I have purposely avoided all those terms which might make thee mistake any common salts, stones, or minerals for it. I advise thee withal to beware of all vegetables and animals: avoid them and every part of them whatsoever. I speak this because some ignorant, sluttish broilers are of opinion that man's blood is the true subject. But, alas, is man's blood in the bowels of the earth, that metals should be generated out of it? Or was the world and all that is therein made out of man's blood as of their first matter? Surely no such thing. The First Matter was existent before man and all other creatures whatsoever, for she is the mother of them all. They were made of the First Matter, and not the First Matter of them. Take heed, then: let not any man deceive thee. It is totally impossible to reduce any particular to the First Matter or to a sperm without our Mercury, and being so reduced it is not universal but the particular sperm of its own species, and works not any effects but what are agreeable to the nature of that species: for God hath sealed it with a particular idea. Let them alone, then, who practise upon man's blood in their chemical stoves and athanors, or, as Sendivogius hath it, *in fornaculis mirabilibus.*

They will deplore their error at last and sit without sack-cloth in the ashes of their compositions.

But I have done. I will now speak something of gener-ation and the ways of it, that the process of the philosophers upon this matter may be the better understood. You must know that Nature hath two extremes and between them a middle substance, which elsewhere we have called the middle nature. Example enough we have in the creation. The first extreme was that cloud or darkness whereof we have spoken formerly. Some call it the remote matter and the invisible chaos, but very improperly, for it was not invisible. This is the Jewish *Ain Soph* outwardly, and it is the same with that Orphic night :

"O Night, thou black nurse of the golden stars."

Out of this darkness all things that are in this world came, as out of their fountain or matrix. Hence that position of all famous poets and philosophers—that "all things were brought forth out of night". The middle substance is the Water into which that night or darkness was condensed, and the creatures framed out of the water made up the other extreme. But the magicians, when they speak strictly, will not allow of this other extreme, because Nature does not stay here : where-fore their philosophy runs thus. Man—say they—in his natural state is in the mean creation, from which he must recede to one of two extremes—either to corruption, as commonly all men do, for they die and moulder away in their graves ; or else to a spiritual, glorified condition, like Enoch and Elijah, who were translated. And this—they say—is a true extreme, for after it there is no alteration. Now, the magicians, reasoning with themselves why the mean creation should be subject to corruption, concluded the cause and original of this disease to be in the chaos itself, for even that was corrupted and cursed upon the Fall of man. But examining things further they found that Nature in her generations did only concoct the chaos with a gentle heat. She did not separate the parts and purify each of them by itself ; but the purities and impurities of the sperm remained together in all her productions, and this domestic enemy prevailing at last occasioned the death of the com-pound. Hence they wisely gathered that to minister vege-tables, animals or minerals for physic was a mere madness, for even these also had their own impurities and diseases, and required some medicine to cleanse them. Upon this *adviso* they resolved—God without all question being their guide—to practise on the chaos itself. They opened it, purified it, united what they had formerly separated and fed it with a twofold fire, thick and thin, till they brought it to the immortal extreme and made it a spiritual, heavenly body. This was their physic, this was their magic. In this performance they saw the image of that face which Zoroaster calls the pre-existent countenance of the Triad. They perfectly knew the *Secundea* which contains all things in her naturally, as God contains all things in Himself spiritually. They saw that the life of all things here below was a thick fire, or fire imprisoned and incorporated in a certain incombustible, aerial moisture. They found, moreover, that this moisture was originally derived from heaven, and in this sense heaven is styled in the Oracles : "Fire, derivation of fire and food of fire."

In a word, they saw with their eyes that Nature was male and female, as the Kabalists express it : a certain fire of a most deep red colour, working on a most white, heavy, salacious water, which water also is fire inwardly, but outwardly very cold. By this practice it was manifested unto them that God Himself was Fire, according to that of Eximidius in *Turba* : "The beginning of all things," saith he, "is a certain nature, and that eternal and infinite, cherishing and heating all things". The truth is, life—which is nothing else but light—proceeded originally from God and did apply to the chaos, which is elegantly called by Zoroaster "the fountain of fountains and of all fountains, the matrix containing all things." We see by experience that all individuals live not only by their heat, but they are preserved by the outward universal heat which is the life of the great world..Even so truly the great world itself lives not altogether by that heat which God hath enclosed in the parts thereof, but it is preserved by the circumfused, influent heat of the Deity. For above the heavens God is manifested like an infinite burning world of light and fire, so that He overlooks all that He hath made and the whole fabric stands in His heat and light, as a man stands here on earth in the sunshine. I say then that the God of Nature employs Himself in a perpetual coction, and this not only to generate but to preserve that which hath been generated ; for His spirit and heat coagulate that which is thin, rarefy that which is too gross, quicken the dead parts and cherish the cold. There is indeed one operation of heat whose method is vital and far more mysterious than the rest ; they that have use for it must study it.

I have for my part spoken all that I intend to speak, and though my book may prove fruitless to many, because not understood, yet some few may be of that spirit as to comprehend it. "Spacious flame of spacious mind," said the great Chaldean. But because I will not leave thee without some satisfaction, I advise thee to take the Moon of the firmament, which is a middle nature, and place her so that every part of her may be in two elements at one and the same time. These elements also must equally attend the body, not one further off, not one nearer than the other. In the regulating of these two there is a twofold geometry to be observed —natural and artificial. But I may speak no more.

The true furnace is a little simple shell ; thou mayst easily carry it in one of thy hands. The glass is one and no more ; but some philosophers have used two, and so mayst thou. As for the work itself, it is no way troublesome ; a lady may read the *Arcadia* and at the same time attend this philosophy without disturbing her fancy. For my part, I think women are fitter for it than men, for in such things they are more neat and patient, being used to a small chemistry of sack-possets and other finical sugar-sops. Concerning the effects of this medicine I shall not speak anything at this time. He that desires to know them let him read the *Revelation* of Paracelsus, a discourse altogether incomparable and in very truth miraculous. And here without any partiality I shall give my judgment of honest Hohenheim. I find in the rest of his works, and especially where he falls on the Stone, a great many false processes, but his doctrine of it in general is very sound. The truth is he had some pride to the justice of his spleen, and in many places he hath erred of purpose, not caring what bones he threw before the schoolmen, for he was a pilot of Guadalcanar and sailed sometimes in his *rio de la recriation*.

But I had almost forgot to tell thee that which is all in

all, and it is the greatest difficulty in all the art—namely, the fire. It is a close, airy, circular, bright fire : the philosophers call it their sun and the glass must stand in the shade. It makes not the Matter to vapour—no, not so much as to sweat. It digests only with a still, piercing, vital heat. It is continual and therefore at last alters the chaos and corrupts it. The proportion and regimen of it is very scrupulous, but the best rule to know it by is that of the *Synod* : "Let not the bird fly before the fowler." Make it sit while you give fire, and then you are sure of your prey. For a close I must tell thee the philosophers call this fire their bath, but it is a bath of Nature, not an artificial one ; for it is not any kind of water but a certain subtle, temperate moisture which compasseth the glass and feeds their sun or fire. In a word, without this bath nothing in the world is generated. Now, that thou mayst the better understand what degree of fire is requisite for the work, consider the generation of man, or any other creature whatsoever. It is not kitchen fire nor fever that works upon the sperm in the womb, but a most temperate, moist, natural heat which proceeds from the very life of the mother. It is just so here. Our Matter is a most delicate substance and tender, like the animal sperm, for it is almost a living thing. Nay, in very truth, it hath some small portion of life, for Nature doth produce some animals out of it. For this very reason the least violence destroys it and prevents all generation ; for if it be overheated but for some few minutes the white and red sulphurs will never essentially unite and coagulate. On the contrary, if it takes cold but for half an hour—the work being once well begun—it will never sort to any good purpose. I speak out of my own experience, for I have—as they phrase it—given myself a box on the ear, and that twice or thrice, out of a certain confident negligence, expecting that which I knew well enough could never be.

Nature moves not by the theory of men but by their practice, and surely wit and reason can perform no miracles unless the hands supply them. Be sure then to know this fire in the first place, and accordingly be sure to make use of it. But for thy better security I will describe it to thee once more. It is a dry, vaporous, humid fire ; it goes round about the glass and is both equal and continual. It is restless, and some have called it the white philosophical coal. It is in itself natural, but the preparation of it is artificial. It is a heat of the dead, wherefore some call it their unnatural, necromantic fire. It is no part of the matter, neither is it taken out of it ; but it is an external fire and serves only to stir up and strengthen the inward oppressed fire of the chaos. But let us hear Nature herself, for thus she speaks in the serious romance of Mehung.

> After putrefaction succeeds generation and that because of the inward, incombustible Sulphur that heats or thickens the coldness and crudities of the Quicksilver, which suffers so much thereby that at last it is united to the Sulphur and made one body therewith. All this—namely, fire, air, and water—is contained in one vessel. In their earthly vessel—that is, in their gross body or composition—I take them, and then I leave them in one alembic, where I concoct, dissolve and sublime them without the help of hammer, tongs or fire ; without coals, smoke, fire or bath ; or the alembics of the sophisters. For I have my heavenly fire, which excites or stirs up the elemental one, according as the matter desires a becoming agreeable form.

Now, Nature everywhere is one and the same, wherefore she reads the same lesson to Madathan, who, thinking in his ignorance to make the Stone without dissolution, receives from her this check. "Dost thou think," says she, "to eat oysters, shells and all ? Ought they not first to be opened and prepared by the most ancient cook of the planets ?" With these agrees the excellent Flamel, who, speaking of the solar and lunar Mercury—and the plantation of the one in the other, hath these words : "Take them therefore," saith he, "and cherish them over a fire in thy alembic. But it must not be a fire of coals, nor of any wood, but a bright shining fire, like the Sun itself, whose heat must never be excessive but always of one and the same degree." This is enough and too much, for the secret in itself is not great but the consequences of it are so—which made the philosophers hide it. Thus, Reader, thou hast the outward agent most fully and faithfully described. It is in truth a very simple mystery and

—if I should tell it openly—ridiculous. Howsoever, by this and not without it did the magicians unlock the chaos ; and certainly it is no news that an iron key should open a treasury of gold.

In this universal subject they found the natures of all particulars, and this is signified to us by that maxim : "Let him who is not familiar with Proteus have recourse to Pan." This Pan is their chaos or Mercury, which expounds Proteus —namely, the particular creatures, commonly called individuals. For Pan transforms himself into a Proteus, that is, into all varieties of species, into animals, vegetables, and minerals. For out of the Universal Nature or First Matter all these are made and Pan hath their properties in himself. Hence it is that Mercury is called the Interpreter or Expositor of inferiors and superiors, under which notion the ancient Orpheus invokes him : "Hear me, O Mercury, thou messenger of Jove and son of Maia, the Expositor of all things." Now, for the birth of this Mercury and the place of it I find but few philosophers that mention it. Zoroaster points at it, and that very obscurely, where he speaks of his Lynges or the Ideas in these words : "Their multitudes leap upward, ascending to those shining worlds wherein are the three heights, and beneath these there lies the chief pasture. This *pratum* or meadow of the Ideas, a place well known to the philosophers—Flamel calls it their garden and the mountain of the seven metals ; see his *Summary*, where he describes it most learnedly, for he was instructed by a Jew— is a certain secret but universal region. One calls it the Region of Light, but to the Kabalist it is Night of the Body, a term extremely apposite and significant. It is in few words the rendezvous of all spirits, for in this place the ideas—when they descend from the bright world to the dark one—are incorporated. For thy better intelligence thou must know that spirits whiles they move in heaven, which is the fireworld, contract no impurities at all, according to that of Stellatus : "All," saith he, "that is above the moon is eternal and good, and there is no corruption of heavenly things." On the contrary, when spirits descend to the elemental matrix and reside in her kingdom they are blurred with the original leprosy of the matter, for here the curse raves and rules ; but in heaven it is not predominant. To put an end

to this point, let us hear the admirable Agrippa state it.
This is he between whose lips the truth did breathe and
knew no other oracle.

> The heavenly powers or spiritual essences, whiles
> they are in themselves, or before they are united to the
> Matter and are showered down from the Father of Lights
> through the holy intelligences and the heavens, until
> they come to the moon—their influence is good, as in
> the first degree. But when it is received in a corrupt
> subject the influence also is corrupted.

Thus he. Now, the astronomers pretend to a strange
familiarity with the stars ; the natural philosophers talk as
much ; and truly an igorant man might well think they had
been in heaven and conversed—like Lucian's Menippus—
with Jove himself. But in good earnest these men are no more
eagles than Sancho ; their fancies are like his flights in the
blanket and every way as short of the skies. Ask them but
where the influences are received and how ; bid them by
fair experience prove they are present in the elements, and
you have undone them. If you will trust the four corners of a
figure or the three legs of a syllogism you may : this is all
their evidence. Well fare the magicians, then, whose Art can
demonstrate these things and put the very influences in our
hands. Let it be thy study to know their Region of Light and
to enter into the treasures thereof, for then thou mayst con-
verse with spirits and understand the nature of invisible
things. Then will appear unto thee the universal subject and
the two mineral sperms—white and red, of which I must
speak somewhat before I make an end.

In the *PYTHAGORICAL SYNOD* which consisted of
three score and ten philosophers, all Masters of the Art, it is
thus written :

> The thickness or sperm of the fire falls into the air.
> The thickness or spermatic part of the air, and in it the
> sperm of the fire, falls into the water. The thickness or
> spermatic substance of the water, and in it the two
> sperms of fire and air, fall into the earth, and there they
> rest and are conjoined. Therefore the earth itself is

thicker than the other elements, as it openly appears
and to the eye is manifest.

Remember now what I have told thee formerly concerning the earth, what a general hospital it is, how it receives
all things, not only beasts and vegetables but proud and
glorious man. When death hath ruined him, his coarse
parts stay here and know no other home. This earth to earth
is just the doctrine of the Magi. Metals—say they—and all
things may be reduced into that whereof they were made.
They speak the very truth : it is God's own principle and He
first taught it Adam. "Dust thou art and unto dust shalt
thou return." But lest any man should be deceived by us, I
think it just to inform you there are two reductions. One is
violent and destructive, reducing bodies to their extremes ;
and properly it is death, or the calcination of the common
chemist. The other is vital and generative, resolving bodies
into their sperm or middle substance, out of which Nature
made them ; for Nature makes not bodies immediately of
the elements but of a sperm which she draws out of the
elements. I shall explain myself to you by an example. An
egg is the sperm or middle substance out of which a chick is
engendered, and the moisture of it is viscous and slimy, a
water and no water, for such a sperm ought to be. Suppose
Doctor Coal—I mean some broiler—had a mind to generate
something out of this egg : questionless, he would first distil
it, and that with a fire able to roast the hen that laid it. Then
would he calcine the *caput mortuum* and finally produce his
nothing.
Here you are to observe that bodies are nothing else but
sperm coagulated, and he that destroys the body by consequence destroys the sperm. Now, to reduce bodies into
elements of earth and water—as we have instanced in the
egg—is to reduce them into extremes beyond their sperm, for
elements are not the sperm but the sperm is a compound
made of the elements and containing in itself all that is
requisite to the frame of the body. Wherefore be well advised
before you distil and quarter any particular bodies, for
having once separated their elements you may never generate unless you can make a sperm of those elements. But that
is impossible for man to do : it is the power of God and

Nature. Labour then, you that would be accounted wise, to find out our Mercury : so shall you reduce things to their mean spermatical chaos. But avoid the broiling destruction. This doctrine will spare you the vain task of distillation, if you will but remember this truth—that sperms are not made by separation but by composition of elements ; and to bring a body into sperm is not to distil it but to reduce the whole into one thick water, keeping all the parts thereof in their first natural union.

But that I may return at last to my former citation of the *Synod*. All those influences of the elements being united in one mass make our sperm or our earth—which is earth and no earth. Take it, if thou dost know it, and divide the essences thereof, not by violence but by natural putrefaction, such as may occasion a genuine dissolution of the compound. Here thou shalt find a miraculous White Water, an influence of the moon, which is the mother of our chaos. It rules in two elements—earth and water. After this appears the sperm or influx of the sun, which is the father of it. It is a quick celestial fire, incorporated in a thin, oleous, aerial moisture. It is incombustible, for it is fire itself and feeds upon fire ; and the longer it stays in the fire the more glorious it grows. These are the two mineral sperms—masculine and feminine. If thou dost place them both on their crystalline basis, thou hast the philosopher's flying Fire-Drake, which at the first sight of the sun breathes such a poison that nothing can stand before him. I know not what to tell thee more unless— in the vogue of some authors—I should give thee a phlegmatic description of the whole process, and that I can despatch in two words. It is nothing else but a continual coction, the volatile essences ascending and descending, till at last they are fixed according to that excellent *prosopopoeia* of the Stone :

> I am not dead, although my spirit's gone,
> For it returns, and is both off and on :
> Now I have life enough, now I have none.
>
> I suffer'd more than one could justly do ;
> Three souls I had and all my own, but two
> Are fled : the third had almost left me too.

"What I have written, I have written." And now give me leave to look about me. Is there no powder-plot or practice ?

What is become of Aristotle and Galen ? Where are the scribe and pharisee, the disputers of this world ? If they suffer all this and believe it too, I shall think the general conversion is come about, and I may sing :

The Virgin's sign returns, comes Saturn's reign.

But come what will come, I have once more spoken for the truth and shall for conclusion speak this much again. I have elsewhere called this subject "a celestial slime" and the middle nature. The philosophers call it the venerable nature ; but amongst all the pretenders I have not yet found one that could tell me why. Hear me then, that whensoever thou dost attempt this work it may be with reverence—not like some proud, ignorant doctor, but with less confidence and more care. This chaos hath in it the four elements, which of themselves are contrary natures ; but the wisdom of God hath so placed them that their very order reconciles them. For example, air and earth are adversaries ; for one is hot and moist, the other cold and dry. Now to reconcile these two God placed the water between them, which is a middle nature, or of a mean complexion between both extremes. For she is cold and moist ; and as she is cold she partakes of the nature of the earth, which is cold and dry ; but as she is moist she partakes of the nature of the air, which is hot and moist. Hence it is that air and earth, which are contraries in themselves, agree and embrace one another in the water, as in a middle nature which is proportionate to them both and tempers their extremities. But verily this *salvo* makes not up the breach, for though the water reconciles two elements like a friendly third, yet she herself fights with a fourth—namely, with the fire. For the fire is hot and dry but the water is cold and moist, which are clear contraries. To prevent the distempers of these two God placed the air between them, which is a substance hot and moist ; and as it is hot it agrees with the fire, which is hot and dry ; but as it is moist it agrees with the water, which is cold and moist ; so that by mediation of the air the other two extremes, namely, fire and water, are made friends and reconciled. Thus you

see—as I told you at first—that contrary elements are
united by that order and texture wherein the Wise God
hath placed them.

You must now give me leave to tell you that this agree-
ment or friendship is but partial—a very weak love, cold and
skittish. For whereas these principles agree in one quality
they differ in two, as your selves may easily compute. Much
need therefore have they of a more strong and able mediator to confirm and preserve their weak unity; for upon it
depends the very eternity and incorruption of the creature.
This blessed cement and balsam is the Spirit of the Living
God, which some ignorant scribblers have called a quintessence. For this very Spirit is in the chaos and to speak
plainly the fire is His throne, for in the fire He is seated, as
we have sufficiently told you elsewhere. This was the reason
why the Magi called the First Matter their Venerable
Nature and their Blessed Stone. And in good earnest, what
think you? Is it not so? This Blessed Spirit fortifies and
perfects that weak disposition which the elements already
have to union and peace—for God works with Nature, not
against her—and brings them at last to a beauteous specifical
fabric.

Now if you will ask me where is the soul or—as the schoolmen abuse her—the form all this while? What doth she do?
To this I answer that she is, as all instrumentals ought to be,
subject and obedient to the will of God, expecting the
perfection of her body. For it is God that unites her to the
body and the body to her. Soul and body are the work of
God—the one as well as the other. The soul is not the arti-
ficer of her house, for that which can make a body can also
repair it and hinder death; but the soul cannot do this; it is
the power and wisdom of God. In a word, to say that the
soul formed the body because she is in the body is to say that
the jewel made the cabinet because the jewel is in the
cabinet; or that the sun made the world because the sun is
in the world and cherisheth every part thereof. Learn
therefore to distinguish between agents and their instruments, for if you attribute that to the creature which belongs
to the Creator you bring yourselves in danger of hell-fire.
For God is a jealous God and will not give His glory to
another. I advise my doctors therefore, both divines and

physicians, not to be too rash in their censures, nor so magisterial in their discourse as I have known some professors of physic to be—who would correct and undervalue the rest of their brethren when in truth they themselves were most shamefully ignorant. It is not ten or twelve years' experience in drugs and sops can acquaint a man with the mysteries of God's creation. "Take this and make a world"—"Take I know not what and make a pill or clyster" —are different receipts. We should therefore consult with our judgments before we venture our tongues and never speak but when we are sure we understand.

I knew a gentleman who, meeting with a philosopher adept, and receiving so much courtesy as to be admitted to discourse, attended his first instructions passing well. But when this magician quitted my friend's known road and began to touch and drive round the great wheel of Nature, presently my gentleman takes up the cudgels, and, urging all the authorities which in his vain judgment made for him, oppressed this noble philosopher with a most clamorous, insipid ribaldry. A goodly sight it was and worthy our imitation to see with what an admirable patience the other received him. But this errant concluded at last that lead or quicksilver must be the subject and that Nature worked upon one or both. To this the *Adeptus* replied : "Sir, it may be so at this time, but if hereafter I find Nature in those old elements where I have sometimes seen her very busy, I shall at our next meeting confute your opinion." This was all he said and it was something more than he did. Their next meeting was referred to the Greek Kalends, for he could never be seen afterwards, notwithstanding a thousand solicitations.

Such talkative, babbling people as this gentleman was, who run to every doctor for his opinion and follow like a spaniel every bird they spring, are not fit to receive these secrets. They must be serious, silent men, faithful to the Art and most faithful to their teachers. We should always remember that doctrine of Zeno : "Nature," said he, "gave us one tongue but two ears, that we might hear much and speak little." Let not any man therefore be ready to vomit forth his own shame and ignorance. Let him first examine his knowledge and especially his practice, lest upon the

N

experience of a few violent knacks he presume to judge Nature in her very sobrieties.

To make an end : if thou dost know the First Matter, know also for certain thou hast discovered the Sanctuary of Nature. There is nothing between thee and her treasures but the door. That indeed must be opened. Now if thy desire leads thee on to the practice, consider well with thyself what manner of man thou art and what it is that thou wouldst do ; for it is no small matter. Thou hast resolved with thyself to be a co-operator with the Spirit of the Living God and to minister to Him in His work of generation. Have a care therefore that thou dost not hinder His work ; for if thy heat exceeds the natural proportion thou hast stirred the wrath of the moist natures and they will stand up against the central fire, and the central fire against them ; and there will be a terrible division in the chaos. But the sweet Spirit of Peace, the true eternal quintessence, will depart from the elements, leaving both them and thee to confusion. Neither will he apply Himself to that Matter as long as it is in thy violent, destroying hands. Take heed therefore lest thou turn partner with the devil, for it is the devil's design from the beginning of the world to set Nature at variance with herself that he may totally corrupt and destroy her. "Do not thou further his designs." I make no question but many men will laugh at this ; but on my soul I speak nothing but what I have known by very good experience : therefore believe me. For my own part, it was ever my desire to bury these things in silence, or to paint them out in shadows. But I have spoken thus clearly and openly out of affection I bear to some who have deserved much more at my hands. True it is I intended sometimes to expose a greater work to the world which I promised in my *Anthroposophia* ; but I have been since acquainted with that world and I found it base and unworthy ; wherefore I shall keep in my first happy solitudes, for noise is nothing to me. I seek not any man's applause. If it be the will of my God to call me forth and that it may make for the honour of His Name, in that respect I may write again ; for I fear not the judgment of man. But in the interim, here shall be an end.

FINIS

CONCLUSION

WHEREAS the former two texts of this book have dealt principally with the obscure practice of the alchemical art, this text of Vaughan also includes certain of the philosophical and mystical notions peculiar to the alchemists. As I have earlier suggested, the basis of the entire scheme is rooted in that system which is called the Qabalah—something of which I attempted to expound on a previous page, and also at some length in other of my books. This assumption is confirmed by Vaughan himself. The entirety of this book *Coelum Terrae* is based upon Qabalistic implicits. For example, on the second page of the book he says, quoting one of the Qabalistic authorities, that "the building of the sanctuary which is here below is framed according to that of the sanctuary which is above". This is simply a repetition, of course, rather similar to the other Hermetic one that "that which is above is like unto that which is below", and vice versa.

It was upon that philosophical foundation that the alchemists reared their art. Taking the first few lines of Genesis as their guide, they sought to duplicate that vast creative process in the lesser world of man's own nature. "The spirit of God hovered over the great waters of creation." So also the production of the Philosopher's Stone was imagined to be a process not too dissimilar to the creation of the universe. For whatever powers and forces their philosophy posited as existent in the macrocosm, in the universe, just those forces were mirrored and so were operative in the microcosm that was man. The alchemists sought to perform a re-creation in man that was comparable to what, in the vast periods of distant time, God had done with the universe. They sought a differentiation of the myriad elements of the human personality so that the inward spirit could be rendered independent in consciousness of the physical frame. Being thus separated from its vehicle, that

195

spirit could by its own innate divine power gain complete
control of that vehicle and rebuild it in very much the same
way as the waters of creation were manipulated and made
subject to the original creative fiat.

Herein, Vaughan embarks upon a lengthy description of
what in the first book of the Bible is called "the waters of
creation". Other alchemists at other times have given it
different names. They named it Virgin's Milk, the Water of
the Wise, Azoth, Mercury, and the First Material. But few,
possibly, have described it half as eloquently and suggestively
as has Vaughan. He personalizes the entire concept in a very
poetic way, speaking of her as a "pure sweet virgin". In so
far as he gives a description of her, stating that "she yields to
nothing but love and her end is generation", we at once are
enabled to associate the idea with concepts inhering in our
own philosophical scheme of things. First of all, we are able
to identify her with what in the Qabalah is called the
Sephirah named *Binah*, who, in a cosmic sense, is described
as being the Great Mother of all. Another of her attributions
is the Great Sea, that passive plastic base over which the
Spirit of Life originally hovered. Because of the synthetic
nature of the Qabalistic Tree of Life, we are able also to
place other ideas in juxtaposition with this one. Hence when
Vaughan speaks of an active and a passive agent in Nature,
identifying this Pure Virgin whose nature is love with the
passive First Material who is our Qabalistic Great Mother,
we are able to assume that the active agent is what the
Zoharists speak of as *Chokmah*, the Father. His nature is
Wisdom, Power, and Ideation.

These are broad concepts which exist on a cosmic
universal plane—generalizations recapitulating themselves
as particulars within the lesser human cycle. Following the
aphorism that Vaughan uses as the beginning, that the
lesser sanctuary is builded on the same pattern as the greater
sanctuary above, we may assume therefore that these
principles likewise inhere within every human being. Thus
the two agents, passive and active, are part and parcel of
each individual's psycho-spiritual constitution.

His statement that he has experimentally handled the
First Material in itself is not the strange fantastic thing that
it might at first sight have seemed. It is not, because, in a

word, you and I and everybody else in this world has done precisely the same. The only difference is that some have realized their own true natures consciously. Others are in ignorance of it. This statement of Vaughan's, and this interpretation, imputes a very high philosophical level to Alchemy. It is clear from our author that it would be ridiculous to interpret Alchemy in a physical, metallurgical manner.

Quite early in his book he says that there are in this world two extremes—Spirit and Matter. He also proceeds to state that in the middle natures such as fire, air, and water the seed of the spirit is not constant. Like all occult philosophy, the Qabalah speaks at great length of these elements of earth, air, water, and fire. Many are the ways in which we can interpret them. Most commonly held, however, is the view that fire is mind, water emotion, air the vital life energy, and earth the body in which all of these forces operate. Above them, and acting through them, is the Spirit. Other thinkers, however, prefer to consider the elements as so many levels or strata of what is known in this day and age as the Unconscious. Vaughan's idea is that the middle natures of fire, air, and water are only the media which convey that vital spirit from one extreme to the other —from the heights to the depths. It is also added that in the material extreme the seed of the Spirit is to be found. To that sentence Mrs. Atwood has added an additional clause: "in the material extreme, *when it is purified*, the seed of the spirit is to be found". The implication is that Alchemy is a technical process of extracting the seed of the spirit from the gross body in which it has been imprisoned for countless ages. After this separation the seed can be subjected to warmth and light and stimulated into further growth, so that it can begin to exert its own divine nature and power by the reformulation of the vehicles through which it must act. Therefore the building up or the concoction of the Philosopher's Stone is nothing more nor less than consciously reorganizing the material with which one has to deal in life. Reconstructing it in such a way that it really shows forth and manifests the splendour and glory of the ineffable spirit that dwells always in its own abiding city within.

Like all other alchemists, Vaughan too lays great stress

on that secret fire which is to encompass that differentiation. It is by means of fire that the spirit separates itself from the body in which it has been bound and by which it has been blinded. By means of fire the new personality may be built up in conformity with the wishes and dictates of the spirit. In the Chinese text *The Secret of the Golden Flower* we read : "The spirit is thought ; thought is the heart ; the heart is the fire ; the fire is the Elixir." Again it seems incredible that there could be individuals who were so blind to the intrinsic evidence of alchemical writing as to believe the alchemists worked with metals and with furnaces and with coals. For what says Vaughan here? Speaking of this fire, he says, "It is not kitchen fire nor fever that works upon the sperm in the womb, but a most temperate, moist, natural heat, which proceeds from the very life of the mother."

This is good symbolism. The mother, as we have already discovered, is that Sephirah on the Tree of Life named *Binah*, and whilst she has various cosmic attributions she is also by reflection an interior or psychological principle. She it is who works in our interior natures as love, as intuition, as aspiration, and all those higher and finer emotions which we seek to express just a little more easily in our own daily lives. From the psychological point of view she would represent the Unconscious, or more especially what the analytical psychologists call the Anima, that vast sphere of feeling, emotion, instinct, and intuition which lies beneath or beyond our normal awareness.

What is it that proceeds from the very life of the Mother? Again, from the psychological viewpoint, we know that the Unconscious is the receptacle of the libido. We need not interpret libido in the crude sexual way that Freud does, but rather we can speak of it as does Jung. Beatrice Hinkle, who translated Jung's *Psychology of the Unconscious*, gives us in a few words what Jung meant by this libido.

He saw (she says) in the term libido a concept of unknown nature comparable to Bergson's élan vital, a hypothetical energy of life, which occupies itself not only in sexuality but in various physiological and psychological manifestations such as growth, development, hunger, and all the human activities and interests.

Now, in the Qabalah the active agent in opposition to the passive agent is *Chokmah*, Will and Wisdom. When we apply these principles to the human being there is of course no spatial concept involved, for we must not be led astray by the formal glyph which shows *Chokmah* to exist opposite *Binah* on the Tree of Life. These principles are interior principles, operating within. So *Chokmah* is, from one point of view, our libido. Therefore the fire of the alchemists is libido, the internal fire—the Will, the Superior Will which Blavatsky has elsewhere defined as the power of the Spirit in action. The heat arising from the very life of the mother is none other than the power of *Chokmah* arising and welling up from the Unconscious depths of the psyche. The awakening of the Will therefore to renewed activity is the crucial experience of the Spagyric Art. In one of the Golden Dawn documents entitled "Man, the Microcosm" we are told that "in the Adept death can only supervene when the Higher Will consenteth thereto, and herein is implied the whole Mystery of the Elixir of Life".

Our text says of the fire that "it is in itself natural, but the preparation of it is artificial". This we have already understood from our perusal of the former texts. And Vaughan goes on to remark that "it is not part of the matter, neither is it taken out of it, but it is an external fire and serves only to stir up and strengthen the inward oppressed fire of the Chaos". Here we are back once more on familiar ground. In occultism there can be no initiation—that is, the commencement of a new interior life—in a candidate or aspirant without an initiator. This process has been somewhat described in the magical section of Chapter Eight. In the mesmeric art it is the magnetism projected upon the patient by the magnetizer which enables the former to pass regressively, as Mrs. Atwood suggests, through the many phases of his historical and evolutionary development back to his long-forgotten life in Reality. Where psychological clinical work is concerned, it is the influence of the analyst which assists the analysand to throw off, through understanding, his infantile and other ignorant modes of reaction towards life, thus coming to know and of course to express what he really is. All these systems, therefore, while expressing the necessity of an inward development, point to the necessity of some extraneous force or personality, which answers to the external fire, to awaken the individual into enlightenment.

I do not wish to comment at too great length upon this *Coelum Terrae* of our Welsh Alchemist. I feel that enough has already been said in commentary upon the other two very important books to enable the individual to see herein very great significance. I have dwelt at great length on earlier pages with three different approaches, three different possible interpretations of the alchemical mystery. All yield a vast store of illuminating material to assist us in our comprehension of what the Alchemists meant. In this present text I believe we have a synthesis of all these three possible approaches. Here and there one finds statements which can only be interpreted along certain lines. By combining them, however, the entire text and the entire subject, which would otherwise be utter obscurity, emerge into the broad daylight of comprehension and understanding.

It is not difficult to realize what Vaughan's feeling is about alchemy. Nor will we experience any perplexity in understanding on what particular plane he himself interprets it. All we are asked to do is to apply ourselves just a little in meditation and reflection upon his statements. Do this in the light of the material we have uncovered above, and Alchemy at once reveals itself to us and discloses the golden treasure which it has concealed. Not only so—and this is most important—but at once something in us begins to stir, to awaken slowly into a new life. It seems as though the mere attempt, if it be accompanied by sincerity and devotion, to fathom and unravel these mysteries brings about in our own inner souls something of that divine transmutation which it is the object of Alchemy to accomplish. And while from all we have said it seems that the alchemists required the stimulus of an external fire in order to arouse the internal, I am quite convinced that the individual who attempts to divine the significance and subtle implications of Alchemy is doing two things.

Not only will he acquire some intellectual knowledge of what Alchemy is, but he will at once awaken, partially at any rate, his own internal fire. This will, to use mystical phraseology, eventually kindle the Light within him.

There are those in the universe, so the great archaic traditions of Mysticism run, whose task is to watch over mankind and to assist in the initiation of the race. They, we are told, never refuse the training of those made ready by life and by experience. How do they become aware of suitable individuals whose training they may further? These guardians or custodians of the secret knowledge find and select their students because with their spiritual vision they perceive the light emanating from that particular individual. It is a commonplace in occultism that surrounding each individual is a magnetic light-sphere, which glows with different colours corresponding to the status of that individual. Likewise it is susceptible to changes induced by will, thought, and feeling. So far as the student is concerned, he himself inexorably draws to his sphere the initiator, who will be to him as the external fire which will fan the dormant inner spiritual fire into a flame—a flame that is both creative and destructive. It is destructive to the coarse grosser elements of his constitution, but stimulating to that spiritual sperm which has been dormant for the countless ages of time.

It has been written in a book which nowadays possibly we are prone to ignore, *The Light on the Path*, that "when the disciple is ready the teacher appears". Let us not therefore be saddened or dejected by our lack of immediate knowledge of our own divine natures. Our task is not so much to worry ourselves as to the final implication of the alchemical art. That is something we must take in our stride, leaving it until such time as we have further and greater knowledge.

Meanwhile we have much work at hand. By reflection, by study, by deep meditation upon these mysteries, we can make our light glow from within. By an ineluctable process of magnetic attraction we will be drawn to, and likewise draw to us, the presence of just those students or teachers who will further our growth in the direction of self-knowledge and self-transmutation.

The Alchemists themselves have promised that divine aid is always forthcoming to those who in all sincerity and humility do even no more than study their writings. In one sense we can see why this should be so. For, as power awakens power, and as light does expel the darkness, so by assimilating the written word of their wisdom, their illumination, and

their undoubted spiritual experience, we awaken within
ourselves spontaneously a reflection of what it was that
blessed them.

Really, the process is not too dissimilar to the ordinary
process of initiation. For example, in the Lodge or Temple
where once the rites of initiatory magic were celebrated,
initiation was accomplished by hardly more than the candidate being bathed in the presence of, or the magnetism emanating from, an advanced initiator who was illuminated and
knew how to stir up the spirit within him.   On an earlier
page I have described how, in the elemental initiations of
that magical organization called The Hermetic Order of the
Golden Dawn, the evocation of the powers of the elements—
whatever they actually may be—had the effect of arousing
the elemental bases of the candidate, of exciting the various
levels of his Unconscious psyche. Mere contact suffices.

A similar process on another plane is narrated byMadame
Blavatsky in *The Secret Doctrine*. There she describes how men
lacked mind in the early days of primitive evolution. The
thinking principle had not yet been developed. It is her
theory, and she quotes from innumerable sources to further
her contention, that it was by the contact of nascent humanity with beings of a superior mental evolution that Mind was
reflected into the brain of man. How that came about we do
not know, and I hardly need to labour the point. I am simply
concerned at this moment in pointing out that in the contact of one mind with another, of one class of function with a
superior function, the one may be assisted and elevated into
a similar superior function.   In this instance the initiator
at the beginning of the path upwards to the Light can well
be hardly more than a text. In such a text we have the living
dynamic thought of great adepts, great initiators. What they
have recorded as being an experimental path to surmounting Nature, as a way to the discovery of ourselves, to the
transmutation of the gross lead of humanity into the pure gold
of spiritual realization and divine action, can be for us
exactly as if we had entered into direct communion with their
own natures.

I have a theory, and it is only a theory, that the adepts
of all time—the saints, the Boddhisattvas, call them by what
name you will—in having achieved the spiritual heights that

they did achieve, left an indelible impress on the *Anima Mundi*, the Soul of the World, what Jung has called the Collective Unconscious. At great length this master psychologist has spoken of primordial archetypes or archaic images that exist in the Unconscious of the Collective psyche. I believe that, because of what they have done, these great beings become identified with these archetypes, or themselves become other primordial images. Their spiritual liberation identifies them with the celestial substratum shared by all men alike. The energy involved in such an attainment sets into motion powerful currents of impulse and ideation which work their way, gradually and slowly, through the unconscious levels of the mass into the consciousness of the individual. Thus changes occur to an individual here and an individual there without his actually being aware of the process involved in the incubation of ideas. These archetypes are the final cause of the instigation of movements based upon apparent personal inspiration. For Jung says, in confirmation, that the Unconscious contains not memories of infancy alone, but ideas as root and stem and seed which may not develop into conscious thought and action for very many years.

How do these root concepts arise in the collective Unconscious sphere ?   I believe, because of the existence and attainment of individuals whose spiritual attainment has a dynamic effect upon the collective sphere.

Since every individual is not only a conscious ego, but also possesses a personal Unconscious, and since, moreover, that personal Unconscious is always in direct contact with, or is a part of, the Collective Unconscious, we as ordinary individuals have direct access at all times to those primordial archetypes, to those great beings. In a word, they exist in ourselves, as mainsprings of our psychic and spiritual life, of which we are not even aware. We have much for which to be grateful to modern psychology. For in confirmation of ancient occultism it has demonstrated to the world that there may exist psychological principles of which we may be totally unconscious.

In these secret psychological or spiritual depths there exist, so I contend, the archetypes of all the saints that ever lived, the divine images of their attainment. Hermes, Basil

Valentine, Sendivogius, Synesius, Khunrath, Eudoxus, and all the other beings we consider great not only in alchemy but also in Mysticism and Religion—these beings have left indelible traces in the deeper parts of our own souls.

Logically, it would follow, then, that by conscious reflection and inspired meditation upon the writings of these beings we have at least one technical method of evocation of the divine in us.˙ Their words, should they take root, will awaken within us the archetype or primordial image which answers by sympathy to the writer thereof.

Since these beings were illuminated, and were abundantly blessed and divinely gifted, it is evident that we too are already, here and now, likewise illuminated. We also are similarly divinely blessed and divinely guided, if only we would realize it. We *can* realize it. They realized it. They were but men even as we are now. They achieved and accomplished the supreme transmutation. We also can achieve. That transmutation already exists in us *now*— at this very moment both of space and time. We are not asked to do the impossible. All we must do is somehow to *realize* it. Then the transmutation is made manifest and clear. As we come to understand that Jesus and Buddha, Hermes, and all the other adepts and saints of all time already exist deep within us, then by reflection upon their lives and their words we make manifest what hitherto had been concealed. We evoke them from within, and become consequently that which we have invoked. The transmutation is effected for all to see. The Philosopher's Stone of divine understanding and knowledge will then have been concocted.